*How to Put
Yourself Across with People*

James K. Van Fleet

How to Put Yourself Across with People

Parker Publishing Company, Inc. West Nyack, N.Y.

PRINTED IN THE UNITED STATES OF AMERICA

ISBN-0-13-430660-0
B&P

TO MY FAMILY

What This Book Will Do for You

SINCE EVERYTHING YOU GET IN LIFE COMES TO YOU either from or through other people, your ability to put yourself across with them will be the main ingredient of your success.

You have to put yourself across with people—you have to sell them on doing what you want them to do if you ever want to get anywhere.

I have listened to hundreds of successful men and women I have met on my speaking tours throughout the country. I make notes every time I talk with a successful person. And I ask lots of questions to find out what he feels has made him a success.

As I've gone over my notes to analyze what these successful people have told me so I could find out why they are so successful, I have found that all of them have one single thing in common, and that is—

THEY ALL KNOW HOW TO PUT THEMSELVES ACROSS WITH PEOPLE

They all know how to put themselves across with their employees—their employers—their customers—their business associates, and they know how to get cooperation and loyalty from them.

They know how to put themselves across with their families, their friends, their neighbors—everyone with whom they come in daily contact.

They know how to sell other people on their ideas. They know how to get along with people. And they know how to get people to do the things they want them to do. When you finish this book, you'll know how to do all these things, too.

No matter what your job is, this book will be a valuable tool for you to use in putting yourself across with people. For instance, you can use it to learn how to chair a PTA meeting; or sell a new idea to an advisory board; win a group of skeptics over to your viewpoint; convince a purchasing committee that yours is the best product; report on a new production technique to a standards committee; teach a method or explain a subject; make a fund-raising speech; persuade a closely knit group to take action; address a convention or union meeting; speak to a group of high level executives; brief a VIP from the head office.

In fact, here are thirteen specific things this book will do for you. It will show you—

1. How to plan an approach to put yourself across with people.
2. How to put your specific proposition across to others.
3. How to get rid of your fear of people.
4. How to make sure you're completely understood.
5. How to break down the barriers of your listener's resistance.
6. How to get immediate attention—and hold it all the way through.
7. How to lead and control small and medium-sized groups.
8. How to use the secrets professionals use to put themselves across with people.
9. How to use special techniques and special procedures—the five senses, audio-visual aids.
10. How to handle special occasions and special people—your employees, your boss, VIP's.
11. How to put yourself across with the people who work for you.
12. How to give orders that always get results.
13. How to get the best out of people.

That's what this book will do for you; that's what it will show you about how to put yourself across with other people. So if you're ready now, let's have at it, shall we?

James K. Van Fleet

Contents

How to Put
Yourself Across with People

1

How to Plan an Approach
that Will Put Yourself Across with People

*Y*OU WANT TO BE ABLE TO PUT YOURSELF ACROSS WITH people so you can gain the benefits of getting them to do what you want them to do. The happy handshake, the courteous smile, and the cheerful greeting won't mean a thing in putting yourself across with others if you don't know what they want. You'll never gain your objectives unless you stop thinking of what you want and think only in terms of *what's in it for them.* So the first technique to use in planning an approach that will put yourself across with others is to. . . .

FIND OUT WHAT PEOPLE WANT
BEFORE YOU START

I don't care what your goal is, whether it's getting someone to chair a PTA meeting, teach a Sunday school class, or make a fund-raising speech, persuade a group to take action, win a bunch of skeptics over to your viewpoint, or convince a purchasing committee that your product is best—*you must find out what people want before you start.* You must be able to show your listeners *what's in it for them.*

When you find out what people want and help them get it, you'll succeed in whatever you're doing. That's the first big secret of putting yourself across with people so you can get them to do what you want them to do. Now let me show you how *not* to use this technique. Then I'll show you what should've been done.

"A couple of days after we moved to San Diego, my wife got a phone call asking her to go from door to door in our new neighborhood to collect for the United Fund drive," Bill West says.

"The woman who called wasn't at all concerned that my wife had three small children to take care of and that we were still unpacking and trying to find everything. She just kept telling Sally how she couldn't find anyone else to do it for her, and how Sally ought to think about helping suffering humanity.

"She never once told my wife how she could benefit by doing this. That woman wasn't at all interested in finding out what Sally wanted. She was concerned only about herself and in meeting some financial goal she'd been given in the United Fund drive.

"Naturally, under the circumstances Sally refused, but I know she would have accepted, even in spite of just getting settled and all, had this woman taken a different approach.

"You see, I install computers for IBM and they move me around a lot. Sally's always been afraid of not being able to make new friends each time that happens. She grew up in an orphanage and she has an abnormal fear of loneliness. Had that woman taken the time to find out what Sally wanted most of all, she'd have been able to get what she wanted, too, but she didn't."

What Should've Been Done?

How should this woman have tried to sell Sally on the idea of helping her out in the United Fund drive? Bill gave it away himself—she should have told Sally how she would benefit by meeting all her new neighbors and how she could immediately gain new friends and become an integral part of her community. She should've used Sally's fear of loneliness as her clinching argument. Then Sally would've no doubt accepted at once for she'd have seen *how she might benefit*. She'd have known immediately *what was in it for her*.

How could this woman have known what Sally wanted? Well, she ought to have at least made an effort to find out by some adroit questioning, but even without doing that, her good common sense should have made her aware of what Sally needed most of all at that particular time.

For instance, have you ever moved before? If you have, then you know how hard it is to tear up all your old roots and your sense of belonging somewhere. You know how sad it can be to leave familiar sights and old friends. And you know how important it is to feel that you belong somewhere—that you're part of some group.

Everyone has a sinking and empty feeling of loneliness when they move to a strange and new place. Sally is no different. Neither am I and neither are you. And this woman should've at least known that much about people before she ever took the phone off the hook to ask Sally to do something for her.

How Do You Find Out What People Want Most?

It's actually quite simple. It's not nearly as hard as it sounds at first. You see, a person might never come right out and tell you in so many words what he wants most of all, even if you were to ask him, so you have to find out in some other way.

Remember how afraid Sally was of loneliness? All the rest of us have fears of some kind, too. *You can easily determine in short order what people want by finding out what they are afraid of. What people want will always be the opposite of what they fear.*

Most advertising that you read in the newspapers and in magazines or that you see on TV is based primarily on fear. If large companies and corporations can use fear and the "what-if-this-should-happen-to-you-technique" as successful sales tools to get what they want, then so can you.

For instance, you buy life insurance because you're afraid you'll die and leave your wife and children penniless. You buy car insurance because you're afraid of becoming involved in an accident and being sued for everything you've got.

People take all kinds of vitamins and pills they don't need simply because they're afraid of getting sick. Big companies sell mouthwashes, shampoos and anti-acid tablets because people are afraid they might have bad breath or dandruff or indigestion.

Cosmetic companies—quite subtly, of course—base their advertising on the fear of loneliness or loss of someone's love and the fear of old age. And on and on and on. You see—

People Always Want to Be Free of Their Fears

But they don't know how so that's your first big clue in planning your approach. Take you, for example. You want certain things in life. By the same token, you are afraid you won't get them. You are not alone. The chief activator for most people is self-centered fear—primarily the fear that they might lose something they already possess or the fear that they will fail to gain something they are trying to attain.

Almost everyone, at one time or another in life, suffers with one or more of these ten basic fears:

1. Fear of failure.
2. Fear of criticism.
3. Fear of not being important.
4. Fear of poverty.
5. Fear of loneliness or loss of someone's love.
6. Fear of loss of liberty.
7. Fear of sickness and ill health.
8. Fear of old age.
9. Fear of death.
10. Fear of the unknown.

Learn How to Use the Silent Skill

No one is going to come right out and tell you point blank what their fears are. You must learn to listen attentively to what the other person says. Listen, not only to what he says, but also, to what he doesn't say. Learn to listen between the lines, too. You'll be amazed at how often the words *fear, afraid, anxious, dread, worry,* and the like are either spoken or implied in the conversation.

It won't be long before you'll become an expert in knowing what people really do want by finding out what they are afraid of. When you know that, you can use the following techniques to plan the rest of your approach to put yourself across with them.

1. Show them *how* to get what they want.
2. You are the teacher, your listener is the pupil.
3. Use this simple format to put yourself across.
4. Double check your statistics.
5. Solve your problems before they happen.

SHOW THEM *HOW* TO GET WHAT THEY WANT

People are always hungry for information that will free them from their fears. If you want to be successful in your own chosen field, then give them that basic information they want so much.

Take the Dale Carnegie course, for example. For years now, hundreds and thousands of people have used it to gain confidence in themselves and in their own abilities. After taking the course, they find that they lose their fear of speaking up in public and expressing themselves before an audience, whether it be to one or two individuals or to a large group of people.

Success Motivation Institute, founded by Paul J. Meyer of Waco, Texas, helps a person get rid of his fear of failure by showing him how to gain confidence in his own abilities so he can give his maximum performance.

"You're in good hands with Allstate; Sears services what it sells; you can be sure if it's Westinghouse," and other sales slogans like these are all geared to give a person what he wants when he buys their products: peace of mind and freedom from fear.

Sharp real estate salesmen, life insurance salesmen, service station operators—in fact, anyone can use this technique to good advantage. Take Harry Collins, a top notch life insurance salesman from Denver, Colorado, for instance.

"I find that the average woman is so afraid of her husband dying and leaving her penniless and helpless that she cannot even talk rationally about life insurance when I broach the subject at first," Harry says. "So in my sales approach, I make every possible effort to put her at ease and to relieve her mind of fear by showing her in dollars and cents how well off she actually is.

"For example, I show her how much social security she'll be entitled to; how much their house is worth; other assets that they have; and finally, just the bare minimum she'll need each month from insurance to keep her home intact and her children together with her. Then I show her how, for just a few dollars more each year in premiums, she can build that minimum up to a reasonable and decent income from additional insurance.

"I never try to sell an insurance policy by scaring the person. As far as I'm concerned, the salesman who uses the *scare technique* is a fraud and a flop. I think people have enough worries already without being harassed with fears about dying. So I try to give my prospects a break.

"To tell the truth, I'll never even attempt to close my sale until I'm convinced that my prospect is completely free from fear. You see, although I use a person's fear to find out what he really wants and to show him what he actually needs, I'll never use it to force life insurance on him. The person who's scared into buying more insurance than he can afford will never keep up his premium payments. He'll let the policy lapse in a few months or so."

You Can Use This Approach with Any Service or Product

Do you sell cars? The average car owner never knows when it's the best time for him to trade his car in on a newer model. He's deathly afraid of making a mistake and losing money. You can remove this fear by giving him the exact information he needs and gain a customer for yourself at the same time.

Or what about the man who wants to invest a little money in the stock market, not for a gamble, but for security. The average person doesn't have the slightest idea of what stocks are safe to buy or the future prospects of any company. If you're a broker-age salesman, you can get rid of this man's fears and indecision by giving him concrete information about the stocks he's interested in.

If you run a filling station, you can use this system of giving a man information to relieve his fears and build up a list of steady customers for yourself. Tom Bales, a service station operator I know, mails a reminder card to his customers every single month to show them the last time they were in to have their car greased and the oil changed. On that card he also indicates the mileage or the date they should next bring their car back into the station to be serviced again.

Is Tom's system effective? I'll say it is. He does this for over a thousand regular customers and they keep coming back to him year after year. I know this works for Tom: I'm one of his steady customers. Why am I? Because his method of reminding me when my car should be worked on gives me complete peace of mind and freedom from fear about it. After all, a car is my second most expensive investment.

So your second technique in planning your approach to put yourself across with people is to tell them what they need to know about your service or your product in a way that will remove their fears. You don't have to be a supersonic salesman or gun for a fast close when you do this. Just give them honest and factual information so they can understand what it is you want them to do and when they should do it. And the best way to do this is to take the position that—

YOU ARE THE TEACHER—YOUR LISTENER IS THE PUPIL

You don't have to talk down to people or assume a condescending attitude to be the teacher or the authority on a subject. After all, your listener expects you to know more than he does if you're telling him about a product or a service in your own specialized field. He came to you looking for advice and answers to his questions so he expects you to give him the information he needs that will help him solve his problems.

I've had successful salesmen in all possible fields tell me that just as long as they stick to *teaching* a person about their service or their product, everything goes well for them. But the moment they stop teaching and start selling, their prospects freeze up on them.

One of the most progressive of all direct sales companies to use this philosophy of teaching the customer about the product is Amway, a company that manufactures a big line of home care items.

The company was founded in 1959 by Jay Van Andel—now chairman of the board, and Richard De Vos—now president of the corporation. They started Amway in the basements of their homes in the little town of Ada, Michigan.

In 1969, their tenth anniversary year, 100 thousand distributors sold more than 85 million dollars worth of Amway products in the United States and Canada!

Today, their national advertising can be seen in *Reader's Digest, McCall's, Parents' Magazine, Life, TV Guide,* and many,

many others. Paul Harvey, the well known newscaster and com-mentator, advertises Amway on the ABC radio network.

How did a company come from a basement business in just ten short years to a nation-wide highly successful corporation selling 85 million dollars worth of their products in 1969?

Well, first of all, they have good products; they'd have to or they couldn't have done it. But so do a dozen other direct sales companies. And that doesn't even begin to count all the other manufacturers who've been established for decades now and sell their goods through regular retail outlets. The biggest key to Amway's success is following the principle of *teaching the customer how to use their products* so the customer can sell himself.

As Jeff Parker, one of their most successful Missouri dis-tributors, says, "They ask us to start out in the business by setting a sensible goal for ourselves of just one sale a day. And the vice president in charge of sales says all we have to do to succeed is simply *teach* the customer how to use the product. Once he knows how to use it properly, he'll sell himself. In short, the Amway slogan is simply this: *Don't Sell . . . Show and Tell!* That system has worked wonders for me."

Be the Authority in Your Own Field

It should be obvious that if you are to be the teacher, you ought to know more about your business than your listener. You must know more about your product or your service than he does, or you cannot possibly be his teacher.

Take those Amway people again, for example. Their distribu-tors keep themselves up to date by attending rallies, seminars, demonstrations, sales meetings, and leadership forums. And it's axiomatic with them that if they can't show a customer how Amway can do the job better than someone else's product—then they don't know enough about it.

You should keep yourself well posted in your own field, too.

Remember this: To be the teacher, you must be the authority. If you're not, your prospect won't listen to you or your proposition. He'll never become your customer nor will he ever do what you want him to do for you.

USE THIS SIMPLE FORMAT TO PUT YOURSELF ACROSS

No matter what your proposition is, your listener will always want to know right away *what's in it for him.* If you don't tell him that in the first five or ten seconds of your approach, you might as well stop talking. He'll have already stopped listening. There are five simple steps in this format you can follow to let him know how he can benefit by listening to you.

Tell Him Immediately How He's Going to Benefit

Let the other person know at once what he's going to gain by listening to you. Don't make him guess. *Tell him what the benefits are.* Don't be vague and non-specific or talk in circles and generalities. Be concrete, definite, and specific about the advantages that soon can be his when he does as you ask him to do.

Just for openers, you could show him how he'll save time, money, and inconvenience by using your product or your service. A reverse way of doing this would be to show him how bad off he's going to be if he doesn't accept your offer. However, this sort of tactic plays directly upon his fears so it's best used as proof or backup for the major benefit you're offering him.

For instance, you might show your prospect how he's going to save money by trading cars right now. If he hesitates, you can always add fuel to the fire by showing him how much money he's going to lose if he doesn't.

Tell Him About Someone Else Who Benefited

No matter how good your product or your service is, no matter how good your approach or how convincing your argument might be, nothing is ever equal to proof like this: "You know Tom Smith who lives over on Elm Street just a few blocks from you? He was in the other day and bought this exact model from me. So I don't want you to take my word for it. You can ask Tom. In fact, I wish you would, for he'll tell you how good it really is."

Proof of how satisfied someone else is with your product or service is one of your most useful tools in putting yourself across with people. Never neglect this valuable technique; always use it.

Successful mail order people never send out a sales letter that doesn't have some kind of testimonial to back up their claims. The time will never come when a testimonial *that has the ring of truth* about it will not be a potent factor in dispelling all doubt in the mind of a hesitant customer.

Show Him How to Gain the Benefits

After you've shown him how someone else gained the benefits, show him the *techniques he can use* to gain those same benefits, too. The best way to do this is to use a *demonstration* or a *practical application* or both. If one picture is worth ten thousand words, then a demonstartion is worth ten thousand pictures, too.

A Demonstration Is Always Used by the Best Salesmen.   It is a sure fire way of keeping your listener deeply interested in what you're doing. Such products as cars, washing machines, dryers, vacuum sweepers, radios, TV sets, and the like lend themselves extremely well to the demonstration technique. Abstract services such as insurance, religion, fund drives, success motivation courses, health services, and so on are usually harder to demonstrate and put across so they require audio-visual aids like records, tapes, charts, diagrams, illustrations.

A Practical Application Is Often Your Clincher.   Here you let your listener become a part of the act. If you're selling washing machines, for instance, you let the prospect run the dials. The same can be said for dryers, radios, TV sets, vacuum sweepers. A car salesman wouldn't dream of trying to sell a car without first letting his prospect drive it.

A demonstration and practical application, after a quick oral opening, is the procedure those successful Amway people always use, by the way. Whatever your product or service, you can tailor your own techniques to these principles and make them work for you.

For one of the finest examples of how to put yourself across to others by using a demonstration and practical application, watch the evangelist, Billy Graham, preach some time. He uses color and movement throughout his entire service to add to the audio-visual aspects of it.

For instance, even though the altar is already surrounded with flowers, a pretty girl brings him a beautiful armful in full view of the audience. He uses a dramatic demonstration by asking those who have already been converted in previous services to stand.

Then he finishes it off with a huge practical application by asking people to come forward at the end of the preaching service and commit themselves to Christ. The organ plays softly during this time to create the proper spiritual atmosphere. Billy Graham is an absolute master of the art of persuasion in one of the most difficult and abstract fields in the world.

Tell Him What It's Going to Cost to Gain the Benefits

In this step, you tell your listener exactly what it's going to cost him to gain the benefits you've been telling him about. Again, let me emphasize that you must be specific and concrete, especially in this step for in most cases you're now reaching for his pocketbook. Vagueness implies that you have something to hide and that you cannot be trusted.

If you're selling him something on the time payment plan, don't tell him twenty dollars a month is all he'll need and then start adding on the sales tax, the excise tax, and the carrying charges. Break it all out for him and make sure he understands how much of his money is going where. Everyone will appreciate your straightforward frankness and honesty. And an amazing number of people will pay cash when they can see for themselves how excessive the interest rates really are.

Even the woman who called Sally could've gotten through to her if she had told her what it was going to cost by saying something about like this: "Sally, I'd like to show you how you can have a wonderful opportunity to get acquainted with all your new neighbors so you can become friends with them. It's the same method I used when I moved here four years ago. All it's going to *cost* you is just a little bit of your time. . . ."

Ask Him to Take Action

After you've told your listener all about the benefits, how someone else gained them, how he can gain them for himself, and how much it'll cost, *ask him to take action.* Leave out this last simple step and you'll never put yourself across with others. You'll not make a sale; you'll make only conversation.

A salesman calls this step the "close," and the most successful ones start closing a sale with their opening statement in the initial approach. That's why I'm discussing it right here even though at first glance it might seem out of place to you.

One of the best salesmen I've ever seen work this technique is Charlie Ryan. He sells Kenmore washing machines for Sears Roebuck. Don't think for a minute that Charlie is "just another washing machine salesman." His income is in the five figure bracket.

Charlie stands beside the escalator exit right at tne entrance to his department. He asks every woman who comes down the escalator the same question: "How'd you like to have a brand new Kenmore washer installed in your home today, ma'am?"

"I save a lot of valuable time that way," Charlie says. "Almost every woman will say 'Yes' to that question. If she does, then I say, 'Let me show you how you can do that.' I turn my back on her and walk straight to my demonstrator. When I turn around again, if she's followed me, then I know she's interested and I start right in demonstrating the new Kenmore and telling her how she's going to benefit by owning it. If she isn't there, I simply go back to the escalator and start all over again with the next woman who comes down."

There are eight salesmen in Charlie's department. Charlie talks to more prospects than anyone else and he sells more washing machines than any other two men put together. Charlie is aggressive; he knows his product. He tells his prospect immediately how she can benefit and he tries to close his sale with his opening sentence. You can easily use the same procedure in your own approach with just a little practice. All it takes is a bit of courage.

DOUBLE CHECK YOUR STATISTICS

Most people are scared to death of the con artist and the glib-tongued salesman who make all sorts of phony promises and exaggerated claims for their services or their products. I've met salesmen who promised me the sky if I'd buy from them. I'm sure you have, too. I steer clear of them for I simply don't trust them.

So don't "blue sky" it for your listener. Just give him the straight facts. Tell him the truth. It always lasts longer than a lie and you don't have to remember what you said. If the car you're selling averages 15 miles to the gallon, then don't tell your prospect he can get 21 or 22 out of it. It's far too easy for him to check with someone else who owns one.

If you exaggerate, sooner or later your lies will catch up with you. Even carelessness about the facts and figures can cause you to lose out. If you're wrong on only one small item, your credibility will be completely destroyed with your listener. So get your facts straight before you start. Confirm all your details and make sure you're on the safe side.

I could best summarize this idea by quoting you the FINA Oil Company's slogan: "Sell a good product, work like the dickens, and don't try to kid anybody."

SOLVE YOUR PROBLEMS BEFORE THEY HAPPEN

There are a variety of methods that successful salesmen use to overcome their prospect's objections. However, for all practical purposes here, one of the best techniques you can use is the "Yes, but . . ." approach.

For example, take Sally's case again. Here's what could've been said perhaps. "*Yes,* I know you're busy unpacking and getting settled, Sally, *but* don't forget the benefits you're going to gain by meeting all these people in your new neighborhood. You're the one who's really going to benefit in the long run. And you'll have a logical reason for ringing your neighbor's doorbell so you can meet her. I know; that's how I got acquainted."

The "Yes, but . . ." technique is a polite but firm procedure. You agree with your listener, but you immediately point out why they should do it anyway. "*Yes,* I know my product costs a little more, Mrs. Jones, *but* it'll last twice as long, the resale value is much higher, and the peace of mind and freedom from fear you'll gain are well worth those few extra dollars you're spending now."

I could not begin to give you here a detailed set of pat rules to follow for no two people are ever exactly alike nor are any two situations ever precisely the same. Besides, if I were to do that, I would only destroy your own capacity for inventiveness and ingenuity. But the basic thoughts and ideas that I have presented here will always work for you.

For instance, you must always find out what people want before you start. You must always show a person what's in it for him before you ask him to take action. These are fundamental facts. So is the idea that people want to be free of their fears. And because these concepts are true, you can always use them as a basis for planning an approach that will put yourself across with people.

With these basic thoughts in mind, then, let's move on into the next chapter so I can show you *how to put your proposition across to others.*

2

How to Put Your Proposition
Across to Others

$\mathcal{I}$N A TYPICAL AND NORMAL DAY YOU'LL NO DOUBT DO SOME,
perhaps all of the following—issue instructions or give orders to
someone; clarify policies and procedures; write letters, memos,
and reports; talk with associates, colleagues, superiors, subordinates; try to influence your friends, your neighbors, even your
own family.

A greater part of your day will be spent in explaining, per-
suading, advising, exhorting, influencing, asking and answering
questions. In brief, you'll spend most of your time trying to put
your proposition across to people so you can get them to do
what you want them to do. And you'll do that primarily by
talking—dealing with people through words.

When you know how to do this effectively, you'll gain at
least these five major benefits—perhaps even more.

1. *You'll get things done* because people will understand what
   you want done—the very first time.
2. *You'll save time* by avoiding mistakes, misunderstanding, and
   needless backtracking.
3. *You'll gain cooperation from people* when you're able to put
   your proposition across to them.
4. *You'll become a clearer thinker* when you force yourself to
   make your ideas clear to others.

5. *You'll get done what you want done* when you know how to put your proposition across to others.

Before I take up the techniques you can use to gain these benefits, I'd like first to cover, quite briefly, four obstacles you can encounter in putting your proposition across to others.

YOU'LL ENCOUNTER RESISTANCE TO CHANGE

The first obstacle you'll run into is resistance to change. All of us are creatures of habit. We hate to change; we hate to disturb the status quo. Your listener is no different. He doesn't want to change the old way of doing things either. Old habits and old ideas are much more comfortable and easier to live with than new ones.

For instance, just suppose you're a brand new supervisor in a department and you've found some areas where some improvements ought to be made. You go to your boss to get his approval on making them. The results you get will depend on how well you present your proposition to him.

If you offer your suggestions to him by showing him first of all how he'll benefit by putting them into effect, he'll listen carefully to you.

But if you don't use this approach, you're likely to get such answers as "We've always done it this way; your timing is bad on this; they just wouldn't go for your idea in the front office; that won't work at all . . . we've tried it before; your idea is too old . . . it's too new . . ."

Remember that the customary way of doing things is hard to give up. Old habits are deeply ingrained in your listener. And unfortunately, most people think a bad habit is better than none at all. To overcome this obstacle of resistance to change, you must show him precisely how he'll gain more by giving up his wornout habits and doing things your way than he will by hanging onto them and doing things the old way.

PEOPLE THINK THEIR OWN THOUGHTS
INSTEAD OF LISTENING TO YOU

This is the second major obstacle that will get in your way. Whenever you're trying to put your proposition or your idea across to someone, you're competing for his attention. Your listener will not give his whole-hearted attention to you all the time. His concentration wanders between what you are saying and his own personal problems and his own pet ideas.

This is especially true if you're going to ask your listener to make a decision of some sort. And the more difficult that decision is going to be, the more hesitant he is to listen to you, even though he knows full well that he should.

Instead of listening closely to what you are saying, he'll be going over in his mind all the reasons why he cannot accept your proposal. The only way you can keep him tuned in on your idea is to keep right on plugging the benefits he'll gain, over and over again, redundant though that might seem to you now.

There are three clues you can watch for that are clear signs you're not getting through to your listener and that you're not holding his complete attention:

Your Listener Asks Unnecessary Questions

If your listener asks a question to which you've previously given the answer just a few moments before, chances are that you're not holding his full attention. If he'd been listening closely to what you've been saying, he wouldn't have had to ask the question that he did.

The right kind of question will show that he's been carefully listening to you and that he's really interested in your proposal. However, the wrong kind of question should indicate the exact opposite to you.

Your Listener Interrupts to Make Irrelevant Remarks

Did you ever tell a joke to someone only to have him interrupt right at the crucial point just before the punch line to introduce an entirely new and unrelated subject? You know you didn't have his attention after all, or he wouldn't have done that.

Don't lose your temper when this happens; keep a tight check rein on your patience. Look at it as an opportunity to gain information for yourself about your listener. What he says or the subject that he introduces can provide a clue to you as to what his real interests are.

His remarks could be triggered by emotions of anger, anxiety, fear, worry, or even joy and happiness. Many times he will start talking about a subject that worries him or that he's deeply concerned about. Listen closely to what he says when he interrupts you so you can turn a temporary disadvantage into a later advantage for yourself.

He Brings up a Point That's Already Been Settled

This is the third indicator that you're not holding your listener's attention. Whenever he asks a question or repeats an argument or an objection that you've already answered, you know that he's somehow missed the original answer you gave him.

He's right back where he was when you first started talking to him. You now have no other choice than to start over, but preferably with a slightly different slant this time so you can put your proposition across to him.

YOU'LL ENCOUNTER WISHFUL LISTENERS

Your third major obstacle to overcome is the wishful listener. Just as we all do wishful thinking, we also do wishful listening.

We tend to hear what we want to hear by distorting and coloring what the speaker said to suit our own purposes.

"People hear only what they want to hear, especially if it's going to cost them money," says George Smith, manager of a Firestone store in St. Louis, Missouri. "Like the fellow who came in here roaring mad the other day saying I'd lied to him about the condition of his tires.

"He'd been in a couple of months before. He was taking a trip to Phoenix, Arizona, and back—a total of more than 3 thousand miles, not even counting any driving around after he got there. He wanted to know if I thought his tires were good enough to make the trip.

"I told him I didn't think they would make it, but that most definitely was not the answer that he wanted to hear. He insisted they could, and he kept after me to say so, but I wouldn't. Finally, I told him they *might* make it, but I sure didn't think so.

"Well, he interpreted they *might* make it to mean that they *would* make it, for that's what he'd wanted to hear me say all the time. He blew out two tires in the desert, ended up with a costly towing bill, and came back here blaming me for lying to him!"

DON'T MAKE UNWARRANTED ASSUMPTIONS

The fourth major obstacle in putting your proposition across to others is one of your own making. Just as your listener can be a wishful hearer, you can also be a wishful talker and assume you know what's going on in your listener's mind, when really, to tell the truth, you don't know at all.

Don't assume that just because he doesn't ask you any questions he understands everything you've said. Nor does his silence mean that he's going to accept your proposition or that he agrees with you on every point. He may not even have heard half of what you've said so far!

There are many, many gaps in conversation and in the exchange of ideas between people. This, of course, if you are a wishful speaker, gives you the perfect opportunity to assume that your listener has heard everything that you want him to hear.

Don't make that mistake. Don't assume the other person is solidly with you all the way. Fill him in. Give him all the details. Ask him questions to make sure he understands what your proposal is and that he knows what you want him to do for you.

These, then, are the four major obstacles that you'll encounter when you're trying to put your proposition across to others. Now let's take up the various techniques you can use to overcome these obstacles and gain the benefits I told you about in the beginning of this chapter.

TELL HIM WHAT'S IN IT FOR HIM

The quickest way to gain your listener's attention so you can hurdle over those four major obstacles is to tell him at once what's in it for him. Tell him the benefits he's going to gain by listening to you.

You'll hear me plug this point of telling your listener what the benefits are over and over again in each and every chapter of this book. But to tell the truth, I can't over-emphasize how important it is to you in putting your proposition across to others. In fact, I can't even emphasize it enough.

Let me illustrate this point to you by showing you how you react yourself. Look at a group photograph, for instance. Where do your eyes go first thing? To yourself, of course.

If you go to sleep and dream, who is always in that dream? You are, without a doubt. Open a newspaper and turn to the stock market page. Which stock quotations do you look at first? Your own, naturally.

The point is, you are self-centered. So am I. So is everyone else. Most all of us respond primarily to those things that affect our comfort, happiness, well-being, and pocketbook.

You can use this basic truth in putting your proposition across with others by phrasing your message in terms that tell your listener immediately *what's in it for him.* That is always without fail the question that is foremost in his mind.

Don't ask your listener to accept your idea for what it is. Ask him to accept it for *what it will do for him.* For example, if you want your boss to okay a new production method, don't tell him the details of how it's going to work. Tell him how your new system will get rid of injuries and lost time, speed up production, boost morale, and make more money for the company.

Want an employee of yours to use his safety equipment? Don't tell him how much an injured worker is going to cost you. He could care less. Tell him instead about the injuries that can come his way if he doesn't use it.

Take the proposition you want to put across to your listener, no matter what it is, put it in terms of the benefits he'll gain by listening to you, and watch your powers of persuasion grow.

HOW TO ANTICIPATE YOUR LISTENER'S OBJECTIONS

How can you anticipate the *specific* objections that are apt to be raised against your new idea or your new proposal? By thoroughly and diligently examining it for flaws and defects yourself before you present it to someone else.

For instance, does your proposition require too much money? Will it take too much time? Will it cause the hiring of more people? Does its success hinge on any unproven assumptions? Has anything similar to it failed in the past? If so, why? Do you personally know of any reason why it shouldn't work?

Be honest with yourself. View your proposition as an outsider would. By asking pointed questions of yourself—and then forcing yourself to answer them honestly—you can probe your proposition for weaknesses, and you can modify, alter, and strengthen it until it is virtually objection-proof even before you start.

KNOW EXACTLY WHAT YOU'RE GOING TO SAY

"Amazing as it might sound to you at first, many people are unable to put their ideas across to others simply because they will not take the time nor will they make an honest effort to get their thoughts straight in their own minds," says Richard Brady, a prolific free-lance writer of self-help and self-improvement magazine articles.

"For instance, I do what is commonly called the "art of living" piece. Now my editors don't want articles from me that give advice in broad, general, and abstract terms. That's what they call *preaching* or *sermonizing*. Instead, they want to see specific and concrete techniques that will show the reader how to gain the benefits that I've already promised to him in the title.

"This forces me to know exactly what I'm going to say. My own way of coming up with a salable article is to look around for a rough spot in my own life that needs improvement and then to *give myself advice* in exact 'how-to' steps or methods that will help me correct this defect or get rid of this bad habit.

"If I don't come up with specific techniques—if I don't know exactly how to tell the reader what to do, I know I don't have an article after all. I have no more than just a vague idea."

This is a good approach to use so you can know exactly what you're going to say. *Give yourself advice.* If you can't sell yourself on your own proposition, why should anyone else listen to you? I can assure you, they won't.

So don't settle for some vague and fuzzy idea and then become angry with someone else when you can't seem to make them see your point or understand what you mean.

Fortunately, there is one virtually foolproof way you can test any proposition you have in mind to make sure it is clear before you try to present it to someone else. It is simple enough, but it does take a little time. But when done properly, it will always save you time in the long run. And if you think you're in too much of a hurry to do this, just remember that *the hurrier you go, the behinder you get*.

You see, although you might not become a best selling free-lance writer like Richard Brady, you still need to—

Get Your Proposition Down in Writing

There isn't a single idea in the whole world that can't be expressed in writing. Even Einstein was able to reduce his theory of relativity to a simple mathematical formula.

By the same token, if you can't get your proposition down in black and white, you simply don't have a completely developed idea. The fellow who says, "I know exactly what I want to say, but I just can't seem to put it in the right words," really has no idea of what he means at all.

You must know the details of your own proposition if you expect to be able to put it across to someone else. The very act of finding the right words with which to express yourself will force you to make your thoughts and your ideas clean and clear. And the best way to do this is to get it down in writing.

BE CONCRETE AND SPECIFIC

It's always easier for your listener to visualize specific things and solid facts than it is for him to try to grasp vague and abstract generalities. Take advantage of this fact whenever you have a proposition to put across. Tell your listener in exact and specific words precisely what you want him to know.

Christ was the supreme master of this art of getting people to see His point. When a lawyer asked Jesus who his neighbor was, instead of defining the word in vague and abstract legalistic language, Christ showed him the real significance of it by telling him the story about the "Good Samaritan."

Christ also knew He would never be able to explain in theoretical terms the love of God for man, but He was able to do so in a practical way that was simple and easy to understand, yet at the same time specific and concrete, in His story of the "Prodigal Son."

You can do the same for your listener by painting word pictures so he can grasp your meaning. Let him see and understand what your point is. Don't tell him the moral of your story; show it to him. Give him an example.

Nor should you say, "In a few weeks or so." Say, "In exactly two weeks and three days." Don't say, "I heard that . . . they said . . . someone told me . . ." Instead, say, "John Bowman told me; the production superintendent said; Sally Smith said to do it this way."

"Delay can be costly for us" should be translated into "Delay now will cost us six-hundred and seventy dollars a week." Don't tell a prospect, "You'll save money." Say, "Mrs. Jennings, you'll save eight dollars and twenty-two cents every month by doing it my way."

So don't be fuzzy; be specific and concrete. The next technique will help you do that, too.

CONCENTRATE ONLY ON ONE SINGLE POINT

"One of the fundamentals of good salesmanship is to *concentrate on a single point and not to scatter your fire*," says Henry Martin, a real estate broker in Kansas City, Missouri. "Let me give you an example of what I mean by that statement.

"Several years ago, a manufacturer of electrical equipment wanted to establish a branch plant east of Independence. They asked me to locate a suitable site of 80 acres for them.

"I found the perfect place, some undeveloped farm land owned by three brothers and a sister, all of whom worked and lived in the city. It had been left to them several years before when their parents died. None of them could farm it and all of them wanted to sell it, but *they'd never been able to agree on a single price*. When I heard that, I knew that was my one single point on which I had to concentrate to put across my proposition to them.

"I got an option from each one of them—four options at four different prices. Then I called them all together to discuss the matter. 'Your prices are all too high,' I told them. 'Here's what the corporation will offer you for that ground. This is the price they're willing to pay you.'

"I pointed out this was the first time they'd had an offer for the land and that if they passed it up, it'd probably be the only chance they'd have to sell it for a good many years to come.

"Then I pointed out that *unless they could agree on a single price,* they would never be able to sell the land for as long as they lived. This was the one major obstacle I had to overcome and it was the one single point I concentrated on.

"They had to agree on a single price before they could ever sell. Once I made that one single point clear to them, the rest of my proposition was easy to put across. In the end, they did agree on a single price and sold their land through me."

You should do the same, whether you have one or more listeners. In short, don't scatter your fire. Concentrate on a single point. You'll find it's much easier to be clear and concise, specific and concrete when you do. It's also much easier to put your proposition across to others when you stick to one single point.

HOW TO USE YOUR VOICE EFFECTIVELY

If you'll remember, I said in the beginning of this chapter that you put your proposition across to people primarily by talking—by dealing with people through words. I'd like to spend the rest of this chapter to show you how you can do a much better job of that when you know how to use your voice effectively.

Develop Your Own Voice Quality

"Some voices have a naturally pleasant quality; others do not," says Dr. Carl Atwood, speech professor at Grinnell College in Iowa. "However, even the most ordinary of voices can be made pleasant if the speaker will get rid of such qualities as nasality, hollowness, hardness, throatiness, and worst of all, monotone.

"Your listener can get used to almost any kind of voice, but a monotone has a deadening sleep-inducing effect on him. Inflection of your voice will also provide proper emphasis to your words. It will make your presentation more intelligible and it will help you hold the attention of your listener. There are three ways you can add expression to your voice—change of pitch, change of volume, and variation of the speed or the rate of delivery.

Use a Conversational Pitch.   "If you use a voice pitch that you use in ordinary conversation, you'll find you can talk indefinitely without wearing out your voice. Find the pitch at which you speak with the greatest ease, comfort, and clarity. Then vary this pitch to place the emphasis where you want it. Varying the pitch will break the monotony and add interest to your delivery.

Select the Volume of Voice to Fit the Occasion.   "You should speak loud enough so everyone in your audience can hear you without any difficulty," Doctor Atwood goes on to say.

"This doesn't mean that you must shout. If your voice is too loud, the hearing attention of your listener will actually dull in self-defense.

"A loud voice that is thin and reedy grates on the nerves for it is primarily a rasping, throaty sound. To gain volume without strain, you must speak from the depths of your chest. Take a deep breath and expel the air slowly as you speak. This will add resonance and give character as well as volume to your voice.

Vary the Rate of Speed.   "The rate of speed at which you speak should be governed primarily by the thought or the idea that you are trying to get across to your listener. Of course, complex material must be presented more slowly. Charts, diagrams, and drawings will always slow down your presentation.

"If you are not using audio-visual aids, as a general rule I would say that between 120 and 150 words a minute is a normal speaking rate. If you speak faster than 160 words a minute, your listener could have difficulty in keeping up with you and in grasping the full meaning of what you are saying. If you speak under 90 words a minute, however, you'll usually lose the interest of your listener.

"To sum up this last idea, I would say that too rapid a delivery confuses while an overly deliberate one irritates people."

MAKE SURE YOU ARE UNDERSTOOD

How successful you are in putting your proposition across to others will also depend on how well you are understood. Here are two easy techniques you can use to make sure that you are.

Choose the Proper Words

Since language is the most important tool you can use to put your proposition across, you ought to develop a healthy respect for the power of words. You should always choose your words carefully and develop your sentences clearly and logically.

The right word in the right place is the keynote of effective speech as well as effective writing. You should use the word that has the exact shade of meaning you want to make your thought clear to your listener.

First of all, you ought to use words that are familiar to your listener. Never try to impress someone by using words they don't know. Your job is to clarify—not to confuse. If certain complex or technical terms must be used to get your point across, then use them. Just be sure you define each new word when you use it

Emphasize the Right Word

I've just said that you should choose the right words so you can be understood. But it does no good whatever to pick the right words if you emphasize the wrong ones.

For instance, read the following sentence out loud, emphasizing each time the word in italics. The various meanings that could be implied by your listener from hearing your vocal inflection are enclosed in parentheses after each sentence.

I didn't tell Tom you were stupid. (But someone else did.)

I *didn't* tell Tom you were stupid. (I know you are, but I'm still keeping it a secret.)

I didn't *tell* Tom you were stupid. (However, I most certainly implied that you were.)

I didn't tell *Tom* you were stupid. (But I told everyone else; I figured someone would tell him.)

I didn't tell Tom *you* were stupid. (But I did say that someone around here was. It's not my fault that he finally figured out that it was you.)

I didn't tell Tom you *were* stupid. (I told him you still are.)

I didn't tell Tom you were *stupid*. (I just said I thought you weren't too terribly smart.)

Where you place the emphasis can completely change the meaning, can it not? And what is true of this extremely simple seven word sentence is true of almost everything you say. How you voice your ideas can make the difference between getting your proposition across—or falling flat on your face.

So remember—if you want to emphasize the importance of what you are saying, underline your words vocally or put them in italics. Monotony breeds boredom. Use vocal ups and downs and word emphasis to keep your listener alert and attentive.

THINK WHILE YOU SPEAK

Speaking is not a purely mechanical procedure. Your words should not only be spoken clearly and distinctly, but they should also be grouped properly to form clear and definite ideas.

So you must learn to think while you're speaking. During the slight pause that folows a sentence, formulate the next one in your mind. As you speak, think about what you are saying.

If you are having difficulty finding the right words with which to express yourself, clarify your thinking and improve your presentation by writing out the complete text of what you intend to say. After you've done that, then you can outline the key points of your talk in short but complete sentences.

If you're speaking to an audience from a lecture platform, you should use no more than an outline, however. And you can always memorize key statements and key phrases you use in your talk.

For years I have used small cue cards that I make by cutting 3″ by 5″ index cards in two. The half-card fits perfectly in my hand and I can hold as many as 5 or 6 in the palm at any one time for quick reference to key points.

Most of the time, I never look at them, but I do know they're there in case of a sudden inexplicable lapse of memory. Maybe they're just a security blanket, but those cards are a lot more dependable than a rabbit's foot!

3

To Put Yourself Across with People ...
Get Rid of Your Fear

ONE OF THE BIG BENEFITS YOU'LL GAIN FROM THIS CHAPTER
is freedom from your fear of people. When you've finished it,
and when you put into practice the techniques you'll learn here,
you'll have complete confidence in yourself and in your own
abilities to put yourself across with others. No matter if you're a
salesman, a schoolteacher, a store clerk, or a housewife, you'll no
longer need to be afraid of people.

Emerson once said, "Fear defeats more people than any other
thing in the world." This is true, especially in your daily relationships with other people. But it doesn't have to be that way.
You don't have to hang onto your fears of people any longer
if you don't want to. As a matter of fact, you can get rid of
every single one of them. Here's how:

1. Analyze your fear so you can destroy it.
2. Don't concentrate on what you are afraid of.
3. Do the thing you fear to do.
4. Act as if it is impossible to fail.
5. Develop confidence in your abilities to speak to people.
6. Control what you think other people think about you.
7. Remember: the only thing you really have to fear is fear itself

ANALYZE YOUR FEAR TO DESTROY IT

The first thing you should realize is that the major reason you fear other people is because you are afraid they will criticize you or make fun of you because of what you say or do. And even though the fear of criticism from others is only a man-made devil, it is still the greatest killer in the world.

Your fear of being ridiculed or criticized by others can murder your ambition, initiative, ingenuity, achievement, daring, and self-confidence. Fear of people and what they might say about you or about your ideas and suggestions can cause unnecessary worry, indecision, frustration, procrastination—even eventual failure on your part.

"Your mind has unlimited power to make all your dreams come true and to fulfill your deepest desires—as long as you allow it to work freely," says Dr. Earl Conway, practicing psychologist from Tulsa, Oklahoma. "But there is no other fear that will close a person's mind more quickly and more securely than the fear of criticism, ridicule, or being laughed at. This fear of what people will say about you can stop you before you even get started."

This is so true. The fear of criticism will even influence the kind of dresses a woman buys, the shoes she wears, the style of her hair. It will decide for a man whether his suit is going to have two or three buttons, or if it's going to be single or double breasted. That's how sensitive we all are to being criticized by other people.

For instance, take the employee who trembles every time his supervisor stops to speak to him; the office secretary who shivers in her shoes whenever the boss calls her; the salesman who's afraid he might lose a sale and get chewed out for it; the teacher who worries excessively about making a mistake in front of her class; the junior executive who fears he won't be able to handle

more responsibility; even the company president who frets and
stews about losing his position to some aggressive young subordinate beneath him. All these persons are committing slow
and painful mental suicide simply because of their unreason-
able fears of other people.

Fear Is a Natural Reaction to Any Unknown Situation

Fear is your normal and natural reaction to a new, strange,
and unknown situation. Let's look at a specific example.

Just suppose you want to buy a new car, for instance. But
you're afraid to do that because you lack the proper information
about this situation. You don't know how much your old car
is really worth. Nor do you know how much that new car should
actually cost. What can you do to solve this problem and get
rid of your fear of doing business with that new car dealer? Well,
here's what I always do:

I go to a finance company like Commercial Credit Plan
(they're nationwide) or to my own bank for accurate and up-
to-date information. There I find out the current *Blue Book*
prices on my own car. Please note that I said *prices* for there
are no less than three that you should know.

I get the *wholesale cost* (that's how much the dealer would
pay at an automobile auction for my old car), the *retail cost*
(that's the price he'd sell it to you for after he bought it at the
wholesale auction or from me), and the *average loan value.*

The average loan value will always be less than the wholesale
cost and my banker, Ed Barlow, says that will no doubt be the
starting offer the dealer will make to me for my old car.

Ed also tells me that I should deduct 10 to 15 per cent from
the *window cost* of the car I want so I can arrive at the dealer's
actual new car cost. And he says that the dealer's average markup
on all those fancy accessories will be from 25 to 50 per cent.

Now I've been able to get rid of my fear of a new, strange,
and unknown situation by gaining knowledge about it that I can
use for myself. I am no longer unequipped to do battle with that

new car dealer. I am no longer handicapped by the fear of ignorance.

You can do the same thing yourself. Here are three steps you can use to analyze your fear and throw the light of understanding on it, no matter what it happens to be.

Admit Your Fear

This is the first step you should take in analyzing your fear. Usually it is the most difficult one to take. Just as an alcoholic hates to admit he can't handle liquor or a dope addict doesn't want to say he's hooked, none of us like to admit that we're afraid of something or someone.

We always tend to rationalize to some extent so it's often hard to admit the whole truth, even to ourselves. But an unacknowledged fear is the one that can cause you the most trouble. You know it's there even when you refuse to admit it. Stuffing your ears with cotton won't make the knock in your car motor go away, no matter how hard you try to pretend it's not there.

So just admit to yourself, once and for all, that you do have this specific fear and more than half your problem will be solved. Once you've done that, you can move on to the next technique in analyzing your fear to destroy it.

Ask Yourself Why You Are Afraid

If your heart skips a beat when your boss asks you to step in his office, stop for a moment and make a careful analysis of the reasons for your fear. Ask yourself *why* you are afraid.

Are you afraid he's going to criticize you for something you've done? *Why?* Have you done something wrong? Are you afraid he's going to fire you? *Why?* Are you lazy, inefficient, stupid, dishonest? If not, then there's nothing wrong at all; there's nothing for you to worry about. You're giving yourself stomach ulcers and cardiac flutter for no good reason at all.

Get Your Fears Down in Writing

It is always helpful if you will write down your fears on paper. Force yourself to put them all down in black and white. This will let you see, once and for all, what it is that's bothering you. In a lot of cases, you'll find you have nothing whatever to fear. All you've been doing is making yourself miserable by nursing a vague uneasy feeling of dread that has no real foundation.

DON'T CONCENTRATE ON WHAT YOU FEAR

Fear requires you to have an active imagination. Don't exaggerate danger in your mind. Your imagination can turn fishworms into snakes and lizards into dragons.

"For the thing which I greatly feared is come upon me, and that which I was afraid of is come unto me," said Job.* So take a lesson from his experience. Remember that when you fear anything, that thing is much more likely to find you and harm you.

"As a man thinketh in his heart so is he," wrote James Allen, the 19th century English author, and today his tiny book, *As a Man Thinketh,* containing those words, is a classic.

Time and again it's been proven over and over. *You get what you think about.* Think about love and you will be loved. Think about hate and that's exactly what you'll get—hate. Concentrate on poverty and you will be poor. Nothing can prevent it. If you fear failure and constantly think about it, you will fail. Nothing can stop it. Worry about criticism from others and you will be criticized for your excessive worry will cause you to make mistakes.

To keep these things from happening to you, change your

* Job 3:25.

negative way of thinking to a positive one. *Don't think about what you fear.* Instead, concentrate on the exact opposite of your problem. If you fear failure—concentrate on success. If you are afraid of being poor—think only of wealth and abundance.

Or when it comes to listening to criticism from others, keep this in mind: It is one thing to listen to the advice of a qualified person when you've asked for that advice. But it is quite another when you allow unsolicited adverse criticism from people to cause you to fail. Get rid of your fear of that kind of criticism right now; drive straight ahead to your goal.

DO THE THING YOU FEAR TO DO

Do the thing you fear to do and you will have the power to do it. If you want to be a painter—you must paint. There simply is no other way to become an artist. You can dream all day long about how famous and how successful you are as a painter, but until you pick up the brush and start painting, you will never gain the power to do it.

If you want to be a writer—then you must write. If you want to be an expert swimmer—then you must swim. The same thing can be said for golf, baseball, skiing, salesmanship, science, medicine, music, and so on. You must make the first move yourself. Until you do that, you will never gain the power to do anything.

So if there do happen to be certain things in your life that you actually dread or fear to do, then force yourself to do those undesirable tasks until you've reached the point where you no longer fear to do them. When you are no longer afraid to do them, then you'll know you have complete control over your emotion of fear. And that, incidentally, is the real definition of courage: the *control* of fear. Courage is not the absence of fear as so many people tend to think.

I suppose that speaking in public strikes fear to the heart ot nearly everyone at first. I know I nearly panicked the first time I stood up in front of an audience. My throat was dry; my voice was raspy. My palms were sweaty and my heart was pounding.

But I spoke the first sentence and I felt better. As I continued to speak, my fears began to fade away. Confidence came back to me for as soon as I did the thing I feared to do, I gained the power to do it.

Gert Behanna, an extremely popular author and lecturer, says she used to suffer untold agonies before every one of her talks. But gradually her fear lessened as she kept on speaking until finally she completely overpowered it, simply by doing the thing she was afraid to do. Last year she spoke more than 1,000 times and said her only regret was that a year was only 365 days long.

This particular chapter is based on one of my own favorite lectures. The effectiveness of this idea of doing the thing you fear so you will have the power to do it is well illustrated by all the letters I've received from people who've heard my lecture and put the formula to work for themselves. Let me quote a few:

Walter C., a salesman from Kansas City, Missouri, writes, "After I heard you talk on how to get rid of your fear of people, I felt I could tackle anyone. Yesterday I walked into the office of a really tough purchasing agent—a man I'd always feared and who'd never once given me an order—and before he could say 'No,' I had my samples spread out on his desk. First time I'd ever opened my sample case in his office. He gave me one of the biggest orders I've ever received."

Marjorie D., a housewife from Joplin, Missouri, says, "I was even afraid to invite my friends in for fear I wouldn't be able to keep the conversation going. But after listening to your talk at our church, I took the plunge and held a coffee call for half a dozen of my neighbors day before yesterday. It was a great success. I had no trouble at all keeping things moving along interesting lines of talk. Thanks so much for your help."

Carol R., a bashful little sales clerk from Topeka, Kansas, who works for Sears Roebuck, says, "I was so afraid of the customers I gave them the feeling I was apologizing to them for waiting on them. I was even afraid to come to your talk; I thought someone might see me there and laugh at me. And then I was scared to death to try your formula about doing the thing I feared to do so I would have the power to do it, but I really didn't have much choice. The personnel manager had given me three weeks to get my sales up to par with the other clerks or he was going to fire me.

"The moment I did as you said, I found that I was suddenly speaking to customers with more assurance. My poise and self-confidence increased. I began to answer objections with authority. My sales went up nearly forty per cent last month and there's never been another word said about dismissal. In fact, the assistant store manager has told me a couple of times now to start thinking about taking over one of the clothing departments myself."

Life will improve for you, too, if you'll just remember this one simple idea. Do the thing you fear to do and you will gain the power to do it. If you don't, you will never have the power to do it. Honestly, it's just that simple.

ACT AS IF IT IS IMPOSSIBLE TO FAIL

Not many years ago a man named Henry Land took a photograph of his little girl. She wanted to see the picture right away. He told her that first the roll of film must be taken out of the camera and developed in a darkroom by using certain chemicals.

He explained to her how negatives were obtained and how they were then used to make positive prints. His daughter listened to all this, but the explanation did not satisfy her at all. She wanted to see the finished picture right now.

"If they can do all that in a darkroom, why can't they do it inside the camera?" she said. "It's dark in there, too, isn't it? Why do I have to wait so long to see my picture?"

As Mr. Land listened to his daughter, his mind began to take hold of this revolutionary idea. Why not build a camera that

would produce finished pictures right on the spot? Just because
no one had ever done it before didn't mean it couldn't be done.

Of course, anyone who knew anything at all about photog-
raphy could have given Mr. Land a hundred reasons why this
couldn't be done, but luckily, he didn't know all those reasons,
and you already know the rest of the story. Today you can buy
a Polaroid-Land camera that will do exactly what young Miss
Land asked her father to do that day.

One of the most frustrating situations in all the world is to
be faced with a problem that you *must* but *cannot* solve. This
causes the average person to suffer a complete loss of emotional
security.

Psychologists say that *fear of failure* is a businessman's biggest stumbling block. But this fear of failure is not limited to
businessmen alone. It is also one of the biggest psychological
stumbling blocks everyone else has, too.

The fear of failure usually stems from the fear of criticism.
A man fears failure because he fears ridicule and the possibility of being laughed at or made fun of. That's why an
amateur writer will finish his manuscript, lock it up tight in the
desk drawer, never to mail it off to the publisher.

When he does this, he's not running the risk of failure and
the *humiliation* of a rejection slip. As long as that manuscript
is safe in his desk drawer, he can dream and pretend to be
Hemingway or Faulkner, maybe even Evan Hunter or Truman
Capote.

That's also the major reason unsuccessful salesmen spend so
much time at their desks doing "necessary paperwork," going
on coffee break, or just sitting in the office shooting the breeze
with each other. They're afraid to get out and make a call on a
prospect because they're so terribly afraid of failure.

But to do something is far better than to do nothing, even if
it's wrong. After all, the law of averages will balance things out
for you eventually if you try. All you need to do to be successful is to act as if it is impossible to fail. If you do stumble once
in a while, that doesn't mean you're awkward or clumsy.

For instance, if your son flunks one math test, you wouldn't label him as a scholastic failure or a potential school drop-out. If your daughter fails one spelling test, that doesn't mean she's going to be thrown out of school either. Or if I get a manuscript back with a rejection slip on it that doesn't mean that I'm a writing failure. It simply means that one particular manuscript didn't sell at that one specific moment of time. That's the only interpretation I allow myself to put on it. That, and nothing more than that, for I always act as if it is impossible for me to fail. As long as I do that, I will eventually sell everything I write, whether I do it now, next month, or next year.

DEVELOP CONFIDENCE IN YOUR ABILITIES TO SPEAK TO PEOPLE

Now I'd like to discuss for a few moments how to develop your abilities and your confidence to speak to a large group of people. You say you never talk to large audiences, that you don't address large numbers of persons, that you're not a professional speaker?

That could well be, but when's the last time you *wanted* to stand up and speak your piece in your Sunday school class, yet you didn't do so because you were too afraid? How many people are there in your class? Twenty—thirty—fifty? That's a lot of people to stand up before, right?

Or what about the times you've wanted to express your opinion at a PTA meeting—present your viewpoint to the town council—address a convention or a union meeting—yet you didn't because you were completely overwhelmed with fear. So whether you're a professional platform speaker or not doesn't really matter. It will pay you dividends to lose your fear of speaking in public, no matter how many people are in the group. First of all, let me give you some basic information about your fear of speaking in public so you'll better understand why you are afraid.

You Are Not Alone.   The man who isn't afraid of speaking in public is as rare as a blacksmith or a good cribbage player. St. Louis University conducted a survey of its speech classes and found that over 95 per cent of those students suffer from stage fright both at the beginning and the end of the course.

A Certain Amount of Nervousness Is Useful.   This is how your body prepares itself for this strange, new, and unknown situation. More adrenalin is pumped into your blood stream. Your pulse beats faster, your breathing speeds up, your muscles tense. Don't become alarmed at this; it's just nature's way of doing things.

By understanding the basic physiological functions of your own body, you can keep this normal preparatory nervous tension from developing into uncontrollable panic. That extra shot of adrenalin will help you to think faster, to talk more easily, and to speak with greater emphasis and intensity than under ordinary normal circumstances.

Most Professional Speakers Are Always Nervous at First. Could be you've heard famous TV and movie personalities say they always have a certain amount of stage fright before they go on and that it persists for the first few minutes of the performance. Well, the same thing is true of professional speakers who earn their living by lecturing to the public.

"A certain amount of nervous tension is always present before I speak," says John Erskine. "It lasts through the first few sentences of my talk. This is part of the price I pay for being in my profession; it's an occupational hazard. But if I weren't built that way, I doubt if I'd be a professional lecturer."

John is an old-timer in this business. He's traveled over a million miles and spoken to more than a million people during his highly successful career and he's still going strong.

He's also a member of the speech faculty at the University of Iowa, holds a B.A. in speech from Florida Southern College, an M.A. in speech from Ohio State University, yet he says he still gets nervous before he walks out on the platform.

So don't worry too much about this kind of nervous tension; it's quite normal and to be expected.

One Reason You're Afraid Is You're Not Used to Doing It. There is a lot of difference between this normal nervous tension almost all good speakers have and a deep fear and dread of speaking in public.

Practice makes perfect in speaking before the public, just as well as in learning to drive a car, dance, play the guitar, or ride a bicycle. So at the risk of being montonous, I will say to you once more, "Do the thing and you will have the power to do it." And the more you do it, the better you'll become at doing it. Now let me give you a few simple secrets the professionals use in their own public speaking.

Don't Memorize Your Talk Word for Word

There's nothing wrong with memorizing certain key phrases, but to memorize your entire talk is to invite disaster. If you for only one split second forget where you are in your talk, you're dead!

The best way to memorize (if you must) is to memorize only certain key points. However, let me also say that if your talk has a natural continuity, just as a schoolteacher's day might have a normal set routine, even that will become unnecessary since you can easily move from one idea to the next. All you need do is arrange your ideas in a logical sequence before you talk.

Rehearse Your Talk First

This one point often marks the major difference between the professional public speaker and the amateur. By the same token, it usually separates the successful performance from the unsuccessful one, too.

One extremely successful and colorful speaker, Harvey Freeland, who's in the advertising business, is constantly in demand to speak at Kiwanis luncheons, Rotary Club breakfasts, Chamber of Commerce meetings, etc. I asked Harvey why; here's what he says:

"I test my ideas for a new talk in everyday normal conversation with my friends and associates. Instead of wasting time talking about the weather or politics or gossiping about my neighbors, I use my coffee break or lunch period to say something like this: 'Sam, I sure had a funny thing happen to me the other day. I'd like to tell you about it.'

"I watch his reactions closely as I tell him the story. If it registers well, I know I have the nucleus for a new talk. He never realizes I'd been rehearsing with him. As far as he's concerned, we've just had a pleasant conversation."

You can test your ideas the same way Harvey does. Or you can rehearse your talk in front of a mirror or give it to your wife or son. It's always good to get a reaction from both sexes before you firm up your speech in its final format.

I personally prefer to dictate into my tape recorder. A lot of mistakes I didn't hear when I spoke come back to me magnified when I listen to myself.

Know Your Subject and Stick to It

One of the main reasons the Great Atlantic and Pacific Tea Company has been so successful through all these years is that they always "stick to the grocery business."

By concentrating on selling groceries and only groceries they have become experts in their chosen field. They've proven they know their business. How successful have they been in doing this? Well, they started in 1859, and they've been going strong ever since. They're the world's largest food retailer, although they are second in total retail sales of all kinds. Only Sears Roebuck is ahead of them, and Sears sells a lot more than groceries to be able to hold down that coveted first place.

So take a lesson from the Great A&P. Don't try to know everything about everything. It can't be done. Learn your own subject and stick to it. Then you can be an expert, too. Remember that you're an expert only as long as you stick to your own line.

Concentrate Only on the Job to Be Done

"It is impossible for a man to lose all his fear of battle," says Colonel Edward Gann. "But he'll tend to forget it, at least temporarily, if you can get him to take his mind off himself and concentrate *only* on the job to be done."

The same thing is true of speaking in public. Forget yourself and concentrate only on your subject. If you start worrying about errors of grammar or the possibility that you might come to the end of your talk before you've actually covered all your material, you can destroy your self-confidence even before you start. Just concentrate on your message and you'll make it through to the end in good shape.

Use the Four S's of Superior Speaking

The four S's of superior public speaking can be nut-shelled for you like this:

1. Stand up.
2. Speak up.
3. Shut up.
4. Sit down.

And since there's nothing I can add to amplify that for you, I won't.

CONTROL WHAT YOU THINK OTHER PEOPLE THINK ABOUT YOU

Not only is it important to control what you think about, as I've already said, but it is also important to *control what you think other people think about you*.

For instance, if your boss looks at you and frowns or if he sounds a little gruff in the morning, that's no reason for you to think that he's thinking about firing you. He probably had a few cross words with his wife about the household bills before he came to work.

"I hear remarks like this every single Sunday," Reverend Charles Harmon says. " 'We were in Kansas City last Sunday,' Mrs. Jones tells me. 'We went to church up there. I wouldn't want you to think we were down at the lake or something like that.' To tell the truth, I didn't think that at all. Frankly, I didn't even notice she was absent until she called my attention to it!"

So you see, to worry and fret and stew about what you think other people think about you is a complete waste of time. Learn to control that tendency and you'll take another huge step toward getting rid of your fears of people.

THE ONLY THING YOU REALLY HAVE TO FEAR IS FEAR ITSELF

During the 1930's the United States was plunged into a deep depression primarily because of fear. Money ceased to circulate; business came to a standstill. Banks were afraid to loan money; farmers and small businessmen went bankrupt. College professors stood on street corners and sold apples. People of all kinds stood in long bread lines. And all this primarily because of fear.

Then, showing the same kind of courage that had helped him win his fight with polio, President Franklin D. Roosevelt, in his 1933 inaugural address, said, "This great Nation will endure as it has endured, will revive, and will prosper . . . *the only thing we have to fear is fear itself.*"

So don't weigh yourself down with fears that don't even exist. Simply get rid of the ones you already have; that will keep you quite busy enough.

If you will sincerely follow these few simple guidelines for putting yourself across with others, and if you'll practice them every day, you'll soon be able to get rid of your fear of people.

At the very least, you'll have it under control and to control your fear is far better than allowing your fear to control you.

So with that final thought firmly in your mind, let's get on to the next subject—that is, *how to make sure you're understood* when you communicate.

4

How to Make Sure You're Understood

O NE OF THE TOUGHEST PROPOSITIONS YOU'LL EVER COME up against in putting yourself across with people is making yourself understood in your writing. If you're an executive, supervisor, businessman, salesman, teacher, preacher, politician —whoever or whatever you might be—chances are you'll find yourself writing more and more letters, memos, inter-office correspondence, and reports.

Tell me now, is your writing clear, concise, to the point, and easy to understand? Or is it fuzzy, vague, non-specific, and hard to read? Does what you say on paper ever cause other people to fumble the ball and make mistakes? Before you make up your mind about this for sure, let me ask you these four questions:

1. Do you ever have to write another letter or memorandum to explain what you said in the first one?
2. Do you ever receive any telephone calls or letters asking you to clarify your original letter?
3. Do you ever let your letters set overnight, read them again the next morning, and wonder what you actually meant?
4. Do you ever start a letter over and over again, only to end up in complete frustration, because you just can't seem to say what you really want to say?

If you answered "Yes" to any one of these four questions, this chapter will help you; you'll benefit by reading it. And although my major emphasis here is on your writing, it will also help you in your speaking ability to put yourself across with others, for the techniques I'll give you here are useful for both.

If you'll follow my simple and easy recommendations in this chapter, you'll benefit in general by saving time, duplication of effort, misunderstanding, and hard feelings. People will understand what you want them to do and do it, and that's the purpose of putting yourself across to them in the first place, now isn't it? Not only that, you'll also gain these three specific benefits for yourself:

You'll Better Your Chances for Promotion.   If you're in a company or a corporation, your way with words on paper may well be the major factor in your getting ahead. If the man next to you writes reports and letters that are more easily understood than yours, he'll be tagged for promotion long before you are. But if you learn to handle yourself in writing and if you know how to put yourself across with people in your letters, you'll be the one who's promoted first.

Your Letters Can Sell You to Others.   To many of the people with whom you deal, your letters are you. The only way some persons can size you up as an individual is by what you say on paper. Many times, your letters can either make you or break you.

Well Written Letters Can Save You Money.   This is especially important to you if you're in business for yourself. A couple of years ago, the average cost of a one page business letter was estimated to be about $2.50. Today, with the inflation we have, who really knows what the true cost is? Whatever it is, it's too much to do it more than once.

Now then. I've used the rest of this chapter to show you the techniques of writing clearly so you can be sure you're understood. For your convenience, I've divided it into three main parts:

1. How to plan your writing.
2. How to make your meaning clear.
3. The 4-S Rule.

The first part, *how to plan your writing,* deals almost entirely with *what* you're going to say. The second part, *how to make your meaning clear,* shows you *how* to say it, while the last part, *the 4-S Rule,* is a summary type of guideline that can be used throughout all your writing to keep it simple and easy to understand.

HOW TO PLAN YOUR WRITING

Lay a Foundation

"The effective writing of magazine articles is based on adequate preparation—the selection, analysis, and organization of ideas," says Harold Ingram, an associate editor with the *New York Times Magazine.* "The free-lance article writer doesn't live who can make a living just by sitting down and writing something off the top of his head.

"In other words, the writer must lay a solid foundation for his writing by his thinking. His preparation may take hours, days, perhaps even months, depending on the size and scope of his article, but no matter how much time it takes, it will still be the most important part of his total effort.

"Preparation will require him to think the piece through bit by bit before writing it. It will make him find the answers to the time-honored questions of *who, what, when, where, why, how.*"

Identify Your Reader

The next step in planning your writing is to identify your reader. You'll be able to put yourself across with others successfully only when you use words and ideas that your readers can understand easily.

And whether they read you loud and clear or not will depend upon their own knowledge and experience—not on yours. As

John W. Harlan, my high school English teacher, always used to say, "A good vocabulary is far better for catching than it is for pitching."

If you're writing for a general and wide distribution—say, for instance, a corporation letter to all employees or a company letter for the bulletin board—you should pitch it at the educational level of the great middle bracket of your readers. But let me give you fair warning right now. Their reading skills and abilities of comprehension might be far less than you actually believe.

You might be quite surprised to find out, for instance, that most best selling books are written at a grade school level. Dr. Benjamin Spock wrote his widely sold book, *Baby and Child Care,* in a simple conversational style. And even though Dr. Spock talks about a great many complicated problems of child health care, he still manages to keep his book at an eighth grade educational level.

Harper Lee wrote her Pulitzer Prize winning novel, *To Kill a Mockingbird,* at a fifth grade reading level. *Exodus,* by Leon Uris, is only one grade higher—the sixth grade.

John Steinbeck, a Nobel Prize winner, wrote all his novels in extremely simple language. Samples taken from page after page of his books test fifth, sixth, and seventh grade.

Even the novels of such literary greats as Somerset Maugham, Sinclair Lewis, and Ernest Hemingway or the more recent works of J. D. Salinger, John Cheever, and Truman Capote all test easy reading for high school freshmen.

To sum up this idea for you, I can tell you that if you want to write a "best seller," you'd best keep it at an eighth grade level, preferably even lower. And the best rule of thumb that I can give you that will help you achieve that goal is—

Never use a word of three or more syllables,
   If a word with one or two will do.

Even if your readers are all technical people, you should surround your heavy technical and scientific language with light and simple one and two syllable words like *make, do, give, get, work, play.*

And if what you write is also intended for untrained people, then you absolutely have no other choice in the matter. You will have to use simple, uncomplicated, and non-technical language whether you like it or not.

"The trouble here in our plant is that most of our directives and memorandums that are written for our own people are all composed at college graduate levels of readability and comprehension, although men of modest education and background —the production line employees—must take the final action on them," says Ralph James, plant manager of the Springdale Rubber Company in Kansas City, Missouri.

"Whenever I find a department foreman or a production supervisor trying to explain some directive to one of our rank-and-file employees, I know the writer didn't do his job properly."

In preparation for your writing, then, always remember to ask yourself first: "Who is my reader going to be? Who must read and understand and take action on this?" The answer you give yourself should have a great bearing on your ideas as well as the words you use.

Know What You Want to Say

This certainly sounds obvious enough, doesn't it? Yet, haven't you yourself received letters and directives that go on and on and on, forever circling their target, but never really zeroing in on it?

Vernon Lemon, an instructor in business correspondence with Mid-America Business College in Cedar Rapids, Iowa, tells his students how to know what to say.

"The first unbreakable rule of effective business writing is to know what you want to say," says Vernon. "If you have to, make some notes first so you'll know what you're doing. By arranging your thoughts on paper in order of their importance, you will actually be organizing your letter.

"Psychologists tell us that we spend nearly 95 per cent of our waking moments thinking about ourselves and what we want. So if you're at a loss as to how or where to begin, then start by spotlighting your reader's wants and needs, his interests and desires. Then you know he'll want to read your letter.

"You see, the best way you can keep your reader's attention on what you are saying is to *use the 'you' approach*. Actually, all you need do is translate your usual *I* or *me* approach into *you* terminology. Of course, it's impossible for you to get rid of all the *I's* and *me's* in a business letter. And that's probably not even desirable, for whenever you use personal pronouns, you're forced to keep your writing on an informal, personal, and friendly basis. Just watch where you place your emphasis.

"To tell the truth, all you need do is think in terms of your reader's interests and the *'you' approach* will take care of itself. Just tell him what the benefits are and how he can gain them for himself. If you can't tell him how he's going to benefit, you're not ready to start writing your letter yet."

Know How to Say It

Not only must you know what you're going to say, but you must know how to say it. Most of your letter writing will fall into three main categories: (1) *to direct*, (2) *to inform*, (3) *to persuade*. All three of these will be concerned with *who, what, when, where, why,* and *how,* but your emphasis will differ each time.

For instance, a directive usually says *what* has to be done; an informative letter will tell the reader *how* to do it; a persuasive letter shows the reader *why* he ought to take action.

Remember though, whether you're issuing a directive, sending out information, or trying to persuade someone to buy your product or to do something your way, you should always tell the reader how the action he takes is going to *benefit* him.

When you can tell a person to do something in such a way that he wants to do what you want him to do, you're really putting yourself across with people.

How to Develop Your Ideas

Although I've found writing to be 98 per cent perspiration and only 2 per cent inspiration, that 2 per cent is still mighty important. Let me tell you about a gimmick I use that helps me gel my own ideas when I'm writing a letter or a memo.

You know those various advertising contests that always ask you to complete a sentence in 25 words or less telling *why* you like or *why* you use a particular product. That's the kind of sentence I use to force myself to come up with good and logical reasons to support my main idea or my main thesis.

You can apply that same formula to all your letters, your directives, and your memos, just as I do, whether you're using them to direct, to inform, or to persuade. Force yourself to give the reasons *why* you want the action taken. For example:

> I want all salesmen to submit their reports on Friday night instead of Saturday morning because: *say WHY in 25 words or less.*
>
> I want you to be home by 10 o'clock Sunday night, Mary, because: *say WHY in 25 words or less.*
>
> I want you to buy my book or car or washing machine or carpeting because: *say WHY in 25 words or less.*

Those 25 words or less should always be phrased in terms of benefits to be gained by the reader. Your reasons *why* should show him the advantages he'll gain when he does as you want him to do.

HOW TO MAKE YOUR MEANING CLEAR

Unless your letters, your memos, your directives, and your reports says exactly what you want them to say, they're apt to become real troublemakers for you. Your job, then, in your actual writing, is to make yourself crystal clear. Here are some of the ways you can do that:

Make Your Writing Brief

"Say what you have to say and be done with it," says Bill Mallory, managing editor of the *Las Vegas Review Journal*. "If you can tell me the whole story in one paragraph, then don't use three or four to do the job. And don't worry if there is a lot of white space left on the paper. If it bothers you that much, then grab a pair of scissors and cut it off!"

Of course, to be brief doesn't mean you should make your letters read like telegrams. You can't get the kind of brevity you want by leaving out the articles *a, an,* and *the.*

But you can get brevity by dividing complex ideas into bite-size sentences and by steering clear of deadhead words and phrases, repetition, and pompous elaboration. Here are four simple guidelines you can use to gain brevity in your writing so you can make your meaning clear.

Use the Active Voice of the Verb

Don't rob your writing of its strength by using the passive voice of the verb if you can use the active voice. When you use the passive voice, it means the subject has something done to it *by* someone. For instance: The ball was hit *by Tom.*

But the active voice means the subject does something to the object: *Tom hit the ball.*

The key word to watch for and get rid of in the passive voice of the verb is the preposition *by,* either spoken *or implied.*

A great many times, you create confusion in what you write when you use the passive voice of the verb. For example, if you write, *This new rule will be explained to all employees,* your readers would have to guess who's going to do the explaining. But to keep this from happening, you could have easily said: *The safety director will explain this new rule to all employees.*

Ninety-five per cent of the time your writing will be simpler, shorter, stronger, and to the point when you use the active voice of the verb instead of the passive.

Take a Direct Approach

You do not need to be a grammarian to recognize a good sentence. After all, the first requirement of grammar is that you focus your reader's attention on the meaning you want him to get. If you take care to make your meaning clear, your grammar will usually take care of itself.

Learn to express your ideas immediately and directly. Unnecessary phrases like *it is, there is,* and *there are* weaken your sentences and slow down your reader's understanding. They also tend to put part of your sentence into the passive voice.

"*It is* the recommendation of the production superintendent that this progress report be forwarded to the head office immediately," would be much better said this way: "The production superintendent recommended we send the progress report to the head office immediately."

Change Long Modifiers to Short Ones

This is another way of achieving brevity in your writing. "Mr. Prescott, *who is* the chairman of the board, will preside at the stockholders' meeting," could be made shorter and clearer by saying, "Mr. Prescott, chairman of the board, will preside. . . ."

"Equipment *that is* deadlined" can be shortened to "Deadlined equipment" while "they gave us a month for *accomplishment of the mission*" can be simplified by saying "they gave us a month *to do the job.*"

Break Up Long Sentences

The other day I read this sentence in a leading business magazine: "There is not enough time available for the average corporation executive to do everything that needs to be done so it is necessary for him to determine judiciously the essential tasks and do them first, and then, to spend his remaining time on those items that are of secondary importance."

Now let me show you how the author could have broken this monstrosity up into three short, simple, and intelligible sentences.

"The average corporation executive does not have enough time to do everything he needs to do. He must decide what is essential and do that first. Then he can spend his remaining time on things that are of secondary importance."

HOW TO BE STRONG AND FORCEFUL IN YOUR WRITING

"Verbs are the most important words in any language because they mean action," says Roy Larkin, a copywriter with Fletcher Advertising Consultants of San Francisco.

"Verbs are the voice of command," Roy goes on to say. "They can make your advertising message vigorous and direct or flabby and roundabout.

" '*Go buy* our product now!' is one of the strongest and most forceful ways to say it."

Don't Commit Verbicide

Good strong active verbs are often converted into abstract nouns that cause you to use a weaker passive verb to support and carry your abstract noun. It's almost impossible to use a strong and forceful one-syllable verb like *run, make* or *throw* when you have an abstract noun for the subject.

For instance, a simple and forthright sentence such as *The doctor examined him* is stretched on out into *His examination was conducted by the doctor* when you commit verbicide.

The simple sentence *He decided* swells up into the pompous

statement *The decision was rendered by him.* Watch out for such abstract nouns as examina*tion,* deci*sion,* prepara*tion,* re-peti*tion,* impres*sion,* situa*tion,* dichotomiza*tion,* and others that come from verbs.

When you start using disintegra*tion* for fall apart—penetra-*tion* for breakthrough—condescen*sion* for look down on—in-terven*tion* for come between—discus*sion* for talk about—it's a cinch you're committing *verbicide.*

The majority of abstract nouns end in *-ion, -ance, -ence,* or *-osity,* but as I've been pointing out to you, the most common and bothersome kind ends in *-ion.* So go through your writing and weed out all the words you can that end in *-ion.* It'll do wonders for both your clarity and your style.

To help you get rid of these abstract nouns made out of verbs, and their accompanying passive verbs, I've made up a list for you of more than 50 one-and-two-syllable-verbs that you can use to describe almost any physical movement you can think of. When you use these short simple verbs, it's almost impossible to make your subject an abstract noun. Even if you could, you won't, for the two won't sound right together.

Bear	Catch	Drop	Hurt	Pitch	Set	Stick	Touch
Blow	Come	Fall	Keep	Play	Shake	Strike	Turn
Break	Crawl	Get	Lay	Poke	Show	Take	Walk
Bring	Cut	Give	Let	Pull	Skip	Talk	Wear
Call	Do	Go	Look	Push	Split	Tear	Whirl
Carry	Draw	Hang	Make	Put	Stand	Throw	Work
Cast	Drive	Hold	Pick	Run	Stay	Tie	

Get Rid of Deadheads

In railroading, deadheads are non-paying passengers or empty box cars. In writing, deadheads are words or phrases that add no meaning to your sentences and can, at times, confuse and mud-dle your meaning. Get in the habit of getting rid of all dead-heads in your writing. Here are some specific examples:

Take Steps.   Telling someone to *take the appropriate steps* to do something only means that he should get ready to do it. *Take steps to be ready* simply means to *get ready.*

In Case.   The phrase, *in case of,* is almost always a dead-head. For instance, don't say: *In the case of* Mr. Smith's accident, a report will be made to the safety officer. Say: Report Mr. Smith's accident to the safety officer.

Business correspondence and inter-office memos are usually loaded with deadheads. Let me mention just a few and give you their real meanings as well.

The Importance of This Cannot Be Overemphasized really means its importance already has been overemphasized.

Every Effort Will Be Made usually means no effort at all will be made.

Interpose No Objection means I don't really approve of what you are doing, but I don't want to commit myself in writing.

Numerous Instances Have Been Reported means I can't pin-point the guilty party.

Other Deadheads.   Instead of using the deadheads in this list, use instead the word in parentheses:

Accordingly   (so)
Afford an opportunity   (permit, let)
Along the lines of   (like)
As to   (about)
At all times   (always)
At an early date   (soon)
At the present time   (now)
At your earliest convenience   (as soon as you can)
Consequently   (so)
Due to the fact that   (since, because)
For the purpose of   (for)
For the reason that   (since, because)

For this reason   (so)
From the point of view of   (for)
Furthermore   (then)
Hence   (so)
In accordance with   (by, under)
In addition   (besides, also)
In compliance with your request   (as you asked)
In favor of   (for, to)
In order to   (to)
In the amount of   (for)
In the case of   (if)
In the event that   (if)
In the nature of   (like)
In the near future   (soon)
In terms of   (in, for)
In the neighborhood of   (about)
In view of the fact that   (as)
Inasmuch as   (since, because)
Incidentally   (by the way)
Indeed   (in fact)
Likewise   (and, also)
More specifically   (for instance, for example)
Moreover   (now, next)
Nevertheless   (but, however)
On the basis of   (by)
On the grounds that   (since, because)
Prior to   (before)
That is to say   (in other words)
Thus   (so)
To be sure   (of course)
With a view to   (to)
With reference to   (about)
With regard to   (about)
With the result that   (so that)

Without a doubt you could find more to add to this list, but I can tell you this much: these are the most common ones. If you will clear all these deadheads out of your writing, you won't have any trouble finding the rest of them. They'll stick out like a sore thumb.

Write As You Talk

"I print a lot of circulars and brochures for direct mail advertisers," says Rick Neal, owner of the Mid-West Printing Center in Chicago, Illinois. "Not only do I do the printing, but I usually do most of the writing for my customers, too.

"For some strange reason, many ordinarily good speakers freeze up at the sight of a blank piece of paper. Most people think that you must write differently than you talk, so they end up with pompous and stuffy letters that are a tangled mess of long words, useless phrases, and ambigious wandering sentences.

"If you do insist on using a *special written English,* you can easily defeat your main purpose: that of making yourself understood. That's certain death in the mail order business," Rick goes on to say. "So it's always best to write as you talk; here are a few ways you can do that:

"*Use Contractions.* It's perfectly okay to say *don't, can't, won't, wouldn't,* and the like in your writing. To tell the truth, it's almost impossible to write pompous and stuffy English when you use contractions.

"*Use Colloquial English.* If you use colloquial phrases like *Okay, you bet, bark up the wrong tree, horse of a different color* when you talk, then do the same when you write. Everyone understands you when you talk, don't they? Then they'll understand you just as well when you write if you use the same words.

"*Be Modern.* Don't use old-fashioned phrases like *please be advised* or *reference is made to yours of the 19th. . . .* You wouldn't talk that way, now would you? Then don't write that way.

"*Be Yourself—Not Someone Else.* Don't pretend to be

someone you're not when you're writing a letter. If you're going to be yourself, you'll always use the words that really represent you. Just tell the truth; it's much easier to remember what you said when you do."

THE 4-S RULE

I'd like to wrap this chapter up for you with what I call the *4-S Rule.* The four principles to be followed in this rule are *shortness, simplicity, strength,* and *sincerity.*

The 4-S Rule can be applied to every technique in this chapter. It's sort of an extra insurance policy. You can use it as a check list to make sure you've kept your writing clean and clear and sharp before you stick your letter in the mail box or throw that inter-office memo in your out-box.

How to Insure Shortness *in Your Writing*

1. Don't repeat what was said in a letter you answer.
2. Leave out unnecessary words and useless information.
3. Shorten your prepositional phrases.
4. Don't use nouns and adjectives made from verbs.
5. Don't qualify your statements with irrelevant *if's.*

How to Gain Simplicity *in Your Writing*

1. Know your subject well enough to talk about it naturally.
2. Use short words, short sentences, and short paragraphs.
3. Be compact. Keep related parts of your sentence together.
4. Tie your thoughts together logically so your reader can follow you without getting lost.

How to Give Your Writing Strength

1. Use concrete and specific words.
2. Use active verbs.

3. Give the answer first; then explain if necessary.
4. Don't hedge by being vague and abstract.
5. Get rid of all deadheads and empty words.

How to Achieve Sincerity in Your Writing

1. Be yourself . . . not someone else.
2. Always tell the truth.
3. Admit your mistakes.
4. Don't exaggerate.
5. Don't write down to your reader.

How to Break Down
the Barriers of Resistance

THERE IS NO MAGIC FORMULA YOU CAN USE TO OVERCOME a person's objections and break down his barriers of resistance, even though a lot of people try to tell you there is. They say that if you use certain *selling words,* you'll be able to plant your ideas firmly in your listener's mind. They act as if the use of certain magic phrases will automatically let you put yourself across with others.

Magazines that sell classified advertising promote this idea, too. They say you should always use words or phrases like these to catch the reader's eye: *amazing—new—now—first—free— limited supply—satisfaction guaranteed—how to.*

What they say is true up to a point, but successful mail order advertisers also say that all the *right words* in the world won't sell your product or your service and keep it sold.

Yet those who insist there has to be some magic formula continue to arrange and re-arrange their words. They try varying degrees of emphasis and forcefulness in their approach. They spice their sentences with flowery words and catchy phrases and then wonder why their listener isn't overwhelmed by such a dazzling display of knowledge, enthusiasm, wit, and humor.

But you see, as I've said, *there is no magic formula* for you to use because no two people will ever respond to you in exactly the same way. *Nor are there any just right words as such.*

The words you ought to use are those that are right for you and that fit your own particular personality.

So it doesn't matter very much which words you use, just as long as you keep them simple enough to make your meaning clear to your listener. What really does matter is your listener's level of hearing you.

THE THREE LEVELS OF HEARING

Whenever you talk to someone, you're getting through to him on only one of these three levels of comprehension: *the non-hearing level . . . the hearing level . . . the thinking level.*

The Non-Hearing Level

At this level of comprehension you're not even registering with him. He's not listening to you at all for his mind is concentrating only on what he wants to think about and what he himself is interested in.

Your husband probably uses this level to carry on a so-called conversation with you at times, especially in the evening after he's eaten and has settled down in his easy chair with the newspaper.

He might even lower his paper once in a while, gaze deeply into your eyes, and even talk to you, saying things like, "Yes, dear, you're right . . . I see . . . and then what did she say? . . . you do have a good point there . . . Mm . . . ," but he really isn't listening to you and you know it as well as I do.

The Hearing Level

At this level, your listener is at least remembering some of what you're saying. If you were to stop suddenly and ask him what you've been talking about, he'd no doubt be able to repeat your last sentence or so or tell you what your last idea was.

However, he really hasn't absorbed what you've been saying. As soon as you stop talking, your ideas immediately disappear from his mind for he's not really thinking seriously about them at all.

Professional salesmen usually call this kind of listener "the tire kicker." Fred Owen, manager of Lillard's stereo and hi-fi department in St. Louis, puts it this way: "He's not really listening to you at all. He's probably just killing time, waiting for his wife to do her shopping. The best way he can do that is to watch the ball game on TV. He listens to your sales pitch just to be polite, but the longer you talk, the more he wishes he'd gone for a cup of coffee instead."

The Thinking Level

At this level, your listener is actually interested enough to *think* about what you're saying. And thinking about something is hard work, so when he does think about what you've told him —then you know he's interested.

For to think means to evaluate, to compare your ideas with someone else's, to weigh advantages against disadvantages, to analyze, and to make some kind of decision.

And if you want to put yourself across with people, *you must get your ideas into your listener's mind at the thinking level.* Anything less than this will not be effective.

How can you tell when he's reached this level? Because he'll ask questions, voice objections, and offer resistance to your proposition. So don't become alarmed when this happens; it's nothing to be afraid of.

When your listener presents a counter argument or voices an objection, it simply means you've put a dent in him. He's now maneuvering for a better bargaining position, or he's waiting to see if you can counter his objection. But you can be sure of this: *You've lifted his mind to the thinking level for he's interested in what you have to say.*

And that will be my purpose in the rest of this chapter: *to show you how to get your listener up to this level and how to keep him there.* For it's only at the thinking level that you'll be able to overcome his resistance and put yourself and your proposition across to him.

PEOPLE DON'T LIKE TO THINK FOR THEMSELVES

To think is hard work. To solve problems, to make decisions, the mind must be harnessed and controlled. And it's a known fact that everyone's as lazy as he dares to be and still get by. On his own volition, your listener is not going to listen to you very long on this thinking level. It's too much work for him to do so.

He would far rather let his mind drift off to more pleasant things, to daydream, to think his own thoughts, even to concentrate on his own problems rather than pay close attention to you. So it's going to be up to you to stimulate him into thinking deeply about your proposition.

HOW TO GET HIM TO THINK ABOUT
YOUR PROPOSITION

When you're trying to put yourself across with others, it's not enough just to put your ideas into words for him. Nor does it do any good for you to say to yourself, "Well, I've done my job by telling him about my product; the next move is up to him." If that's your idea of how to put yourself across with people, you'll not manage to do it.

"You need to reach out, touch his mind with yours, and make it work on your proposition," says Carl B. Patterson. Carl is a sales consultant to such leading firms as Ford, Sears, Texaco, Ralston Purina, and many others. He has trained more than ten thousand salesmen in clinics and seminars. He is also the head of Carl B. Patterson & Associates, a nationally recognized sales and public relations counseling service.

"If you're selling something, you haven't done your job at all if you stop at just telling about it, no matter how well you do that," Carl says. "Of course, that's all the average salesman will do. But even when he asks for the order that is still not enough.

"The successful salesman puts his proposition across by *helping* his listener evaluate every single one of the benefits that have been offered to him. And unless you do this—unless you stimulate your listener to think about your offer—you're not going to have a meeting of the minds. In fact, all you're going to ring up on the cash register is the 'No Sale' sign."

YOU CAN STIMULATE HIS THINKING BY ASKING HIM QUESTIONS

When a person offers resistance (either active or passive), or when he objects to your ideas, it's of no use for you to get angry about it. You cannot change his mind by talking louder or faster or by getting all upset just because he doesn't happen to see things your way the very first thing.

The only way you can overcome his resistance, so you can get him to accept your proposition, is to find out *why* he doesn't agree with you. You need to smoke his objection out into the open for you can't overcome it until you know what it is. The information you need to put yourself across with him is locked up tight in his head. The only way you can find out what it is is to ask him questions.

"I don't waste time trying to be subtle," says Calvin Rice, a household appliance salesman for Loring's Appliance Center in Fort Dodge, Iowa. "I come right out and ask her—most of my customers are women—why she doesn't like my product or what there is about it she doesn't care for. Then I take her objection, twist it around, and turn it into a reason why she ought to buy.

"For instance, take that new style dishwasher over there by the door. It has round corners on the inside. Women aren't used to seeing that so that's one feature they almost always object to. But I can take that objection and *boomerang* it into a reason for her to buy. Here's about what I would say to her:

" 'You say you don't like this round inside tub, is that right, Mrs. Smith? Is that your main objection? Well, to tell the truth, this round tub is much more efficient than the old-fashioned kind with square corners on the inside. This round tub will get your dishes cleaner. That's why the designers made it that way.

" 'You see, the square tub on the inside slows down the wash water, Mrs. Smith. Those square corners cause weak and wasteful back surges of water that do no real washing of your dishes at all. In fact, they actually keep your dishes from getting completely clean.

" 'So you see, Mrs. Smith, this round tub is one of the best reasons for you to buy this new kind of dishwasher. No other dishwasher on the market today can get your dishes as clean as this new model right here.'

"But I can't use her objection as a selling point until I know what it is," Carl says in conclusion. "That's why you must ask your prospect questions to uncover his resistance. It's the only way you can ever hope to find out what he really thinks about your proposition."

HERE'S ANOTHER WAY TO USE THE QUESTION

The question is truly an extremely useful tool to use in conversation. Not only can it be used to gather information and overcome your listener's resistance just as Carl does, but it can also be used to transmit information and ideas from you to your listener. Let me give you an example of that so you can see how it's done. Then you can use the technique yourself.

I learned how to use this method from Dutch Whitley, the production superintendent of the Dayton Rubber Company's plant in Waynesville, North Carolina. I was on a working vacation in the Great Smoky Mountains fishing and gathering information on the various paper, textile, rubber, and plastic factories in western North Carolina. That's how I came to meet Dutch.

Dutch always used questions to plant his desires in the heads of his supervisors so he could get them to do what he wanted them to do. But let Dutch tell you how to do it just as he told me:

"We always keep a journal around the clock for we're a 24 hour a day operation here," Dutch says. "It's the first thing I read when I come in the plant in the morning. I want to know what happened during the night. Fact is, the night supervisor never goes home until I've checked out his entries in the journal.

"Most of the time those entries are specific and to the point, but sometimes they get sort of vague and hazy. Then I usually have a session with the night supervisor that sounds about like this:

"I say, 'Charlie, I've been going over some of your entries in the log book and I'm not sure of what you mean in some places. For example, you give me your opinion about conditions on the night shift, but you don't give me any facts to back it up. *Do you realize you're doing this?'*

"Charlie says, 'Gee, Dutch, I've got more to do on the night shift than sit in here and make entries in a book. Besides, I can't see any use of going into details. What you really want is my opinion, right? So I figured I'd shortcut and give you that. After all, I know you've got a lot of stuff to read and plenty of other work to do, too.'

"I say, 'I appreciate that, Charlie, but I still need the facts on which you base your opinion. For instance, you say in several places that morale is low. But you don't say *why.* So I don't know what you're basing your opinion on. In fact, I don't know for sure what you mean by low morale. How low is low? Do you mean the men are griping just a little? Or are they really complaining about something specific? Is the quality of their work slipping? Is production going down? Is this a real crisis or is it just another one of those cycles we go through every spring when everybody wants to go trout fishing instead of working? *Don't you see how defining what you mean by low morale will help me?'*

"Charlie says, 'Well, you might be right, Dutch, but I figured everybody knew what low morale was. And I thought since I'm a supervisor, you'd trust my judgment.'

"I say, 'Charlie, I do have a lot of confidence in you or you wouldn't be the night supervisor. The thing is, though, low morale means different things to different people, so I've got to know what you mean. Let me give you a different example, Charlie. Just suppose I were to tell you I didn't think you were doing a good job. *Wouldn't you want to know what I based my opinion on?'*

"Charlie says, 'I sure would! I'd want to know exactly what you thought I was doing wrong.'

"I say, *'And when you ask me for an explanation, does that mean you don't trust me or that you lack confidence in my judgment?'*

"Charlie says, 'Of course not. But I'd still want you to tell me why you felt that way. I'd be entitled to know that, Dutch!'

"I say, *'But Charlie, isn't that exactly what I'm doing when I ask you to define low morale and to back your opinion up with facts?'*

"Charlie says, 'Gosh, I never looked at it that way before, Dutch. I guess you're right. Okay, I'll try to pinpoint what's wrong for you in my journal entries from now on.'

"Now I know I could have put my foot through the floor and demanded that Charlie give me all the facts. And of course, he'd have to," Dutch says. "But if I did it that way, I'd have to hassle with him every morning about the log book. It takes a little longer this way, but it sure has a more lasting effect."

SEVEN BENEFITS YOU CAN GAIN BY ASKING QUESTIONS

"You can gain seven specific benefits for yourself when you ask questions," says Wesley L. Stevens, Professor of Marketing in the University of Iowa's College of Commerce. "The advantages that I gain by asking my students questions are just as applicable to any other situation, be it a salesman asking questions of his prospect, a businessman of his employee, a doctor of his patient, or a lawyer of his client.

"Just change a few words here and there, modify the emphasis a little, and these same benefits can be yours, too, no matter what you do. All you have to do is substitute the word *customer, employee,* or whatever's appropriate for you wherever I use the word *student.*

"In my classes, I use questions to increase interest, stimulate thinking, reveal attitudes, permit student contributions, reinforce major points of emphasis, check the effectiveness of my presentation, and adjust my instruction to the class. Now let me explain these benefits in more detail for you. Then you'll be able to see quite clearly how you can gain them for yourself.

"**Questioning Increases Your Listener's Interest.**   Interest increases when you can get your listener to participate by asking him questions. My students are always interested in being able to talk themselves. They feel they can contribute more to the instruction if they are allowed to ask questions without restraint and to respond freely to questions posed by me.

"**Questions Stimulate Their Thinking.**   My students are much more alert when I hold them responsible for learning. It stimulates their thinking processes. They will pay closer attention and think more about the subject if they know I'm going to question them on it. When I ask questions, and when I encourage their questions, I know I'm helping to stimulate their desire to learn. You'll find the same thing holds true with your employees.

"**Questions Help Reveal Their Attitudes.**   A student's response to my question will often indicate his interest in the subject, or it will tell me what his general attitude is about it. And his attitude is important to me for I need to know how much motivation he has to learn and understand.

"Questions Permit Student Contributions.   From their own experience or their outside reading, my students will have fresh ideas and new applications of the subject material. I always encourage them to contribute their ideas. Their participation is most desirable for it stimulates their interest and adds variety.

"Questions Let You Reinforce and Emphasize Major Points. Retention of major points of emphasis is made easier by frequent recall. When you ask a question on a particular point, it is plain to see you are emphasizing that idea. Their answers to your questions help reinforce those major points in their minds.

"Questions Let You Check the Quality of Your Presentation. One of the best ways to find out whether your listener understands you or not is to ask him questions. His answers should readily show you just how good your methods, your techniques, and your aproach have been. At the same time, his answers should show you the exact areas where your presentation needs to be improved.

"Questioning Lets You Adjust Your Presentation to the Proper Level.   If you're a teacher, I'm not saying you should lower your standards; you should not. However, it's an old adage that if the majority of the class flunks the course, the teacher— not the student—is at fault. Not only that, it is absolutely useless to assume your listener understands you if he does not. Questions will help you adjust your presentation to the person's rate of learning. If he doesn't understand you, then you have no other choice than to simplify or expand your material. Besides, questions will often reveal misunderstandings that can be corrected right on the spot."

START WITH QUESTIONS THAT ARE
EASY TO ANSWER

You should start out with questions that are easy to answer so your listener will relax and feel at ease when he talks with you. People enjoy giving answers they know are right for it gives them a chance to show how knowledgeable they are.

This is especially true if your listener is a stranger and if you're planning to sell him something—say, a new house or a new car. He'll really be on guard with you in the beginning. Resistance and distrust of people is characteristic of almost all of us when we're doing business with someone we don't know.

Your listener doesn't know whether you'll be hard or easy to talk with. The first few things you say will help him decide that. As Elmer Wheeler, who's often been called *America's Number One Salesman* and whose *Sizzlemanship* methods have been used by more than 250 of America's largest firms, always said, "Your first ten words are more important than your next ten thousand!"

If you're hard to talk to, your listener will become more evasive and withdrawn. Then you press harder to make your point with him and he'll withdraw even more. This becomes a vicious cycle that ends up with no agreement at all between you.

But if you start out with easy questions, his nervousness and fear of you will soon disappear. He'll answer your questions with confidence. You ask him more easy questions. He relaxes even more. Soon you're engaged in a pleasant and fruitful conversation.

A lawyer never presses the witness for an answer to the crucial question the very first thing. A real estate salesman talks first about the number of children, what kind of house the prospect lives in now, how long it takes him to get to work, and the like. A personnel manager interviewing a job applicant asks questions about a man's family, hobbies, likes and dislikes before he starts digging out the hard facts about education, past experience, and other qualifications.

You, too, will have to warm up your listener first so he'll feel comfortable with you. You can't approach him with the bureaucratic iciness of a government census taker or an internal revenue agent and expect him to cotton to you just like that. Just relax; make it easy for both of you.

HOW TO PHRASE YOUR QUESTIONS

Poorly worded questions actually discourage answers and may only confuse your listener. Correctly worded questions will follow these five basic guidelines:

It Should Have a Specific Purpose

Your question should be designed to achieve a definite goal. One question might be used to emphasize a major point. Another to stimulate thought. Still another to arouse interest and make your listener more alert and attentive.

You can use a question to check on your listener's immediate understanding, while a later question on the same point can be used for recall. Instead of asking your listener if he has any questions or not, be more specific. Ask him questions to make sure he understands.

Your Question Should Be Clear and Concise

Your question should be phrased in clear and concise language so your listener can understand what you want. Avoid lengthy questions that take a lot of explanation or clarification. Simply worded questions that are direct and to the point will be understood by your listener and serve your purpose best.

It Should Emphasize Only One Point

Don't ask two questions in one. If your question requires several answers, then break it up into smaller segments.

A Good Question Requires a Definite Answer

Ask your question so that a definite and specific answer will be required. A vague and indefinite question invites a vague and indefinite answer.

Your Question Should Discourage Guessing

Don't use a question that can be answered "Yes" or "No" unless you follow it up with "Why?" This makes the listener explain his answer. Don't use leading questions that suggest the answer to be given either. If your listener's answer does not show whether he understands your question or not, it's a poorly worded question.

HOW TO CONTROL THE INITIATIVE
IN A CONVERSATION

When you ask questions you are controlling the conversation. You are actually leading the other person's thinking in the path you want it to take. You point his mind in a specific direction and then you get him to give you the answer. Your question is, in effect, a request for him to think about the subject that you have chosen to discuss.

Many statements are in reality questions in themselves. "I expected to see you in church last Sunday" really means "Why weren't you there?" "I thought you'd be at the meeting last night" implies "Where were you?"

If you want to get someone to talk about a specific subject, without asking him point blank for his ideas, you can always start out something like this: "George, I don't know what your opinion is on this, but I think . . ." "Jack, I don't know what you think about Senator Jackson, but I've always felt . . ." "Sally, I don't know how you feel about a wife working, but I've always thought . . ." These statements or similar ones are usually all it takes to get the other person into the subject that you want to talk about.

Your own role in this is very misleading. You seem to be the person who's asking for help, advice, or information when you ask another man for his opinion. When you do this, you make him appear to be an expert in the subject. To tell the truth, however, you're taking complete command of the conversation by making the other person talk on the topic you've selected.

A top notch salesman always controls the situation by guiding his prospect's mind. That's why he's a top notch salesman. Let's watch Boyd Turner, a manufacturer's representative for Bell Industrial Tool and Supply Company, as he calls on a potential buyer, Ron Upshaw, in Fort Worth, Texas. Watch how Boyd controls the conversation all the way through with his questions.

> BOYD: "Mr. Upshaw, tests conducted by Southwestern Testing Laboratories show that our ring molds outlast our nearest competitor by at least 25 per cent and our other competitors by two or three times. Yet our price is no higher than theirs. So when you buy from us, you save money. *How do you feel about that?*"
>
> UPSHAW: "Well, of course I would like to save money for the company, but we're all set up with the Superior Brands people right now. They've given us good service. We're satisfied with them."
>
> BOYD: "You say you're satisfied with them. *Does that mean you haven't had any trouble at all with their product?*"
>
> UPSHAW: "Oh, we have a little trouble now and then, but nothing too serious. Besides, they come and replace a broken or cracked ring mold right away. So we can't complain about the service they give us. And you know, nothing's perfect these days."
>
> BOYD: "You're right, nothing's perfect. But my company works hard to keep trouble for the customer down to a minimum. Zero defects, that's us. *How much trouble are you having anyway?*"
>
> UPSHAW: "Oh, not very much, really. But I will say I'm a little disappointed in one thing and that's our replacement purchases. Seems to me we're not getting as much service out of those ring molds as we ought to."
>
> BOYD: "Really? *How much service are you getting from them?*"
>
> UPSHAW: "Well, to tell you the truth, only about eight months."
>
> BOYD: "Eight months is all? Why, that's nearly four

months less than you could be getting with our ring molds. Ours are unconditionally guaranteed to last for at least twelve months. Tell me this, Mr. Upshaw: *Wouldn't you like to extend the life of your ring molds so you could cut down on replacement costs?*"

UPSHAW: "I sure would, but there's more to it than that. I don't want to upset our present system. It'd mean putting out a complete set of new instructions for the production line. The men would have to get used to your product. I don't want them to get all confused and start messing things up."

BOYD: "I can understand how you feel about that, but I doubt if it would happen. If your men knew they were getting a better product to work with, seems to me they'd be happy to change. *Have you ever changed ring molds before?*"

UPSHAW: "Well, yes we have. We started using Superior Brand ring molds about two years ago. Why do you ask that?"

BOYD: "I'm just trying to look at your past record. *How much trouble did you have when you changed ring molds that time?*"

UPSHAW: "Let me think. Actually, there wasn't much trouble at all. Oh, a few times when things went wrong, we blamed it on the new molds, but the trouble was straightened out right away. I sort of think it would have happened anyway."

BOYD: "Then it seems to me you're paying nearly a third more for your present ring molds to prevent trouble that isn't likely to even happen. *Isn't that true?*"

UPSHAW: "I guess you're right in a way. Maybe I am worrying a little too much about a changeover. And I am unhappy with the short production life of our present molds. I did expect more service from them than we're getting. Tell you what, suppose you send me a trial shipment so I can try yours out on one section of the production line. We'll see how they work out."

You can easily see from this how Boyd held the initiative all the way. His first few questions caused Mr. Upshaw to think and to become dissatisfied with the situation. Further questioning showed him the futility of retaining his position. So in the end, he came around to Boyd's way of thinking. You can do the same. Using questions is an excellent way of getting a man to change his position and see things your way.

MAKE QUESTIONING A ROUTINE HABIT

Always remember that you can use questions effectively to break down the barriers of your listener's resistance. Yet at the same time, questions can be used for more than just getting information from your listener. They can also be used to change a person's position, sway his way of thinking, or get him to make a firm commitment, just as Boyd Turner did when he talked with Ron Upshaw.

This kind of questioning is truly a conversational art. Just suppose, for example, you're trying to sell a product or a service or an idea, or simply get the other person to see things your way.

Somewhere along the line you can ask him, in effect, *"If I show you how you can benefit, will you buy my idea?"* He either has to say yes or he has to say why he doesn't want to go along with you.

Either way you force his hand so he has to bring his thinking out into the open for you to see. And either way, you are now in a position to close the sale or to overcome his objection. You could not have done this without your skillful use of questions.

So in your conversations with others, get into the habit of talking less but asking more. When you say something, try to word it in such a way that you'll get a reaction to your statement.

When you're trying to get another person to adopt your line of thinking or to see things your way, you cannot ask indiscriminate questions just at random. This accomplishes nothing; it does not serve to bring two minds closer to agreement.

Ask yourself first: "Exactly what specific information do I need from this person to sell him on my idea?" Then word your questions properly so you can get the information you need.

This will take practice. You don't learn this technique in five minutes. It will require a lot of thinking on your part to come up with the right kind of questions. But it'll pay you rich dividends. The most successful salesmen have mastered this fine art of asking questions. In fact, this ability is a major factor in putting yourself across with people, no matter what your objective is in doing so.

When you get into the groove of constantly asking questions instead of talking just to hear your own voice, you'll find the conversation flows more smoothly and that it's much more stimulating and exciting. Not only that, you'll find your average of getting the other fellow to see things your way will keep climbing higher and higher.

In short, ask questions, and lots of them. It's a simple and easy way to put yourself across with people so you can get what you want.

6

How to Get Immediate Attention— and Hold It

WHY IS IT SO IMPORTANT TO GAIN A PERSON'S IMMEDIATE attention and hold it all the way through your presentation? Well, if you want to be able to sell your listener on your product or your service, if you want to persuade him to accept your idea, your proposition, or your point of view—in short, if you want to gain the benefits of getting him to do what you want him to do—then you must gain his immediate attention and hold it to the very end. You must hold his interest long enough to get him to take action. If you can't do that, you'll never be able to put yourself across with people.

Here, then, are the techniques you can use to gain immediate favorable attention—and hold it to the very end.

PLAN YOUR OPENING STATEMENT

The first thing you ought to think about in planning your opening statement is the status of your prospective listener. Who he is and what he does will help determine where his interests lie and what your general approach should be.

Know Who Your Listener Is

If you're going to make a talk to a group of employees about production, for example, chances are your *slant* and your *em-*

phasis would be much different than if you were going to brief the board of directors. I don't mean to imply that you should talk *down* to subordinates and *up* to superiors. In fact, it's not wise to talk *down* or *up* or even *to* anyone; it's far better to talk *with* him.

However, the point is that the status, the position, or the occupation of your listener will definitely influence the slant of your opening statement. Once you know who your listener is going to be, then you ought to—

Find Out What He's Interested in

Remember how I told you in Chapter 3 that you could determine what a person wanted most of all by finding out what he was afraid of? Now let's look at that same idea from the other side. You see, you can sum up quite well what everybody wants in this way:

> *Every normal person wants to know how to be loved— how to win money or fame or power—and how to stay healthy, the easiest way possible.*

Know What You Have to Offer

Keeping this idea in mind of what everyone wants most of all, now analyze your own product, service, or proposition to determine how you can fulfill one or more of these basic desires of your listener. Let me give you an example of what I mean to help you along.

"Most salesmen will say there are only four reasons for a customer to buy anything," says Peter Updike, general manager of a Kansas City, Missouri, branch store of the giant K-Mart chain.

"The reasons they give are *gain, safety, pride,* and *convenience.* But there's also a fifth one which can at times be more powerful than all the others put together. And that one is *love.*

Let me show you what I mean by that:

"The other day I watched one of our salesmen in the household appliance department demonstrate a dishwasher to a man and his wife. He plugged those four standards benefits of gain, safety, convenience, and pride over and over again and he did it well.

"After a while, the wife left to go to another part of the store. As she left, she said to her husband, 'You decide, dear; it would be nice to have, but I don't know if we can afford it or not, so whatever you do will be all right with me!'

"You know what she was doing? She was opening the door wide open for her husband to walk through. She wanted that new dishwasher in the worst way, but she wanted her husband to make the final decision. Just in case you didn't know, that's a subtle feminine trick women use to get what they want without seeming to ask for it. However, the salesman wasn't able to pick up that cue, so he missed an opportunity to turn the husband into a customer.

" 'You should've told him about one more benefit, Tom,' I said to the salesman afterward. 'It no doubt would've been the clincher for you. You should've plugged the benefit of *love*.'

"Tom looked at me doubtfully. 'How are you going to sell a dishwasher by talking about love?' he said. 'The two don't go together at all.'

" 'Oh yes they do,' I said. 'All you needed to say to him was simply this: *Your wife will love you for it.* That one sentence could've wrapped up your sale for you.' "

MAKE UP AN OUTLINE

Once you've decided what benefits you can offer your listener, then you'll need to show him how he can gain those benefits for himself. One of the best ways to do that is to make up an outline that shows the techniques he can use to gain the benefits that he wants.

You can use any number of good ways to outline your talk. However, I'd like to give you the one I've developed over the years. I've found that it's the most reliable method to use to get immediate attention—and to hold it. The outline itself is so adaptable that I use it as the format for a talk, a magazine article, or the chapter of a non-fiction book.

For instance, when I'm preparing a talk or writing the chapter of a book, I look at that talk or that book chapter as a container of four or five major techniques that will allow my listener or my reader to achieve the benefits I'm offering to him. So the first thing I need to determine are the *benefits to be gained by him.*

If I can't come up with any, then that talk isn't worth giving nor is that chapter worth putting in the book. It's just so much hot air and I throw it out.

Now then. Let me give you that specific outline that I use:

FORMAT FOR A TALK, MAGAZINE ARTICLE, OR CHAPTER IN A BOOK

Benefits to be gained by the reader or the listener

Exactly how you do this is up to you. Your method will depend upon the time or space you have that you can use. So here, rather than discussing specific how-to, let me talk about some of the most common benefits that you should be able to offer your reader or your listener. Once you know what they are, then you can determine how to make up your own opening statement of the specific benefits you have to offer.

1. *Gain.* When you offer a person the chance to make money or save money, you are at the same time counteracting one of his main basic fears: *the fear of poverty.*

2. *Pride.* Appeal to a person's pride and you can counteract three of his basic fears all at the same time: *fear of failure, fear of criticism, and the fear of not being important.*

3. *Convenience.* This benefit is in direct opposition to a person's *fear of loss of liberty.* Who wants to spend two hours a day doing a job if you can show him how to do it in one? Always keep in mind that everyone is just as lazy as he dares to be and still get by.

4. *Safety.* Plug this benefit and you help rid a person of his *fears of sickness and ill-health, old age, death, and fear of the unknown.*

5. *Love.* Love is thought to be the strongest motive of all by most psychologists, but it is often completely neglected by many salesmen. When you push this benefit, you'll help a person combat his *fear of loneliness or the fear of loss of someone's love.* One of the most potent sales closers you can ever use is contained in this one sentence: *Your wife (husband, daughter, son, father, mother) will love you for it!* Remember it please; it's a powerful persuader and a real money-maker.

I'm sure you've already noticed it, but just in case you haven't, these five benefits counter every single one of the ten basic fears almost all of us have at one time or another.

Techniques to be used to gain the benefits offered

1. *List the techniques to be used* as a major subheading in your article or your talk.

2. *Explain each technique* by telling how it works and what it does.

3. *Illustrate the technique.* Show specifically how it worked for someone else, for instance, Jim Green, Sam Smith, Charlie Gray.

4. *Tell the reader (listener) how he can use the technique himself.* Explain how this same technique or its corollary can help him solve his own problems.

5. *Move on to the next technique.*

Summarize the Benefits and Techniques.

If you'll notice, this outline corresponds roughly to the three parts of a talk most speakers use, i.e., *beginning—middle—end.* The three main parts of my outline, however, would be more properly labeled *benefits—techniques—summary*. Let me say a few words about each one of them right here before going on.

Benefits.   Most beginning writers tend to overload the benefit section. They manufacture imaginary benefits because they think quantity makes quality. But it's far better to have only one strong benefit than it is to have five or six weak ones. If there are multiple benefits to be gained, fine. By all means, list them then. But don't fabricate them just to attract attention. Phony benefits are as transparent as a see-through blouse, but not nearly as interesting.

A speaker is also inclined to make the same mistake. He wants his talk to cover everything—to be the ultimate of all talks. But when he tries to do that, he leaves himself empty and with nothing to talk about the next time.

Good salesmen will enumerate certain benefits to be gained by the prospect, primarily to find out where his interests lie. The moment that prospect indicates more interest in one specific benefit than the others, the top-notch salesman will latch onto that one immediately and stick to it from then on.

Techniques.   Now a word about techniques. They should be usable and plausible, concrete and specific. You can't dream up vague and abstract techniques any more than you can dream up imaginary benefits.

For instance, just suppose you were lecturing to young junior management people on how to get ahead in the business world. Each one already knows the basic rudiments of business. Now he's looking for more sophisticated know-how and how-to, advanced techniques for getting better results from his people, his time, and the material and funds he has to work with.

He already considers himself to be a part of the management team, so he doesn't want to hear any vague and abstract pep talks about the goodness and glory of a hard day's work, that he should dress well, that he should try to get along with everybody and so on. He wants meat to chew on. It's up to you to give it to him.

Summary.   The summary or the conclusion can consist of an enumerated list, or even the title of *Points to Remember,* especially if your talk or your writing has been so long and so detailed or complicated and technical that your listener or your reader might have forgotten some of your main points.

However, if it's short, a few minutes or so, you might be better off just to wrap it up with a paragraph type conclusion that can also serve as a short summary for you.

Now let me give you a specific example of how you can make this outline work. Chapter Fourteen of one of my books, *Guide to Managing People,** is called "How to be Liked by Your Employees—and Still be the Boss!" Let me show you now how the outline for that chapter looked in its bare skeleton form in the beginning before I put some meat on its bones. I hope you've already noticed that the title of the chapter is in itself a benefit to be gained by the reader.

HOW TO BE LIKED BY YOUR EMPLOYEES— AND STILL BE THE BOSS!

Benefits to be gained

1. It's a good feeling inside to have people like you—to feel that you're respected, that you're really wanted.

2. You won't have to put on a false front. You can simply be yourself.

3. You won't have to use soft soap and flattery to butter up your employees.

4. You won't have to throw your weight around just to prove that you're the boss.

5. You can just act normal. You won't have to indulge in any of those silly games people play in a useless attempt to impress others.

---

* James K. Van Fleet, *Guide to Managing People* (Parker Publishing Company, Inc., West Nyack, New York, 1968).

Techniques you can use to gain these benefits

1. Set the example to be followed. (But don't worry about someone else's morals when you do. You're the only person whose morals you really have to worry about.)
2. Don't set up your own standards of right and wrong.
3. Don't expect your employees to agree with everything that you say or do.
4. Make allowances for inexperience.
5. Always be considerate.
6. Always be consistent.
7. Give ground on trifles—never on principles.
8. You must see—and be seen. Mingle with your people. (But remember, too, when the boss gets involved too deeply in the employees' work, he's no longer the boss!)
9. Know every employee by name. (Yes, it can be done!)
10. Have the courage to make a decision—to take a risk —to assume the full responsibility.

To Sum It All Up. . . .

This, now, was only the bare outline of benefits and techniques to be used in that chapter. When the chapter was fully fleshed out, it explained each technique in detail, it illustrated each technique by showing how someone else had made it work, and it showed the reader how he could apply the same method or a similar one to solve his own individual problems.

Incidentally, this same outline that I used for that chapter in my book also serves as the basis for a talk that I've given dozens of times to businessmen and executives throughout the country at Kiwanis luncheons, Rotary Club breakfasts, and Junior Chamber of Commerce meetings.

I also hope you've noticed that I didn't choose this chapter just at random to use as an example. I chose it on purpose for it specifically follows the same theme of this book. You see, if you happen to have people working for you, that illustration I gave you is an extra bonus for it shows you (the boss) how to put yourself across with people (your employees).

As I told you, this outline can be used for a talk, a magazine article, or the chapter of a non-fiction book. However, when you use this format for a talk, you need to put a slightly different slant on your opening or your introductory remarks. The thing is, when you're making a talk or trying to make a sale, then you need a strong opening punch line or a "Hey you!" to get him to look your way.

Since you normally have to depend on your voice to attract attention when you talk, unless you're using a vivid demonstration, then you must dramatize your ideas by painting word pictures. The best way you can do that and gain immediate attention with your opening statement in a talk is to—

PROMISE HIM A BENEFIT FOR JUST LISTENING TO YOU

Over the years I have tried a variety of methods to gain immediate attention when I speak to an audience. From that experience I've learned two things *not* to do as well as what to do. Let me first tell you what not to do so we can get that out of the way. I don't want it to be a stumbling block for you.

One thing not to do is never to open your talk with an apology of any kind. You know the sort I mean: "I didn't know I was going to be called on until five minutes ago . . . I never dreamed they'd ask me to speak . . . I'm really not an expert in this field. . . ." Such an opening is a surefire way to turn your listener off.

The second thing not to do is not to open your talk with a funny story or joke. Nine times out of ten it doesn't go over and it gets you off to a miserable start.

On the positive side, the most reliable method I've ever found to get immediate attention is this: *Promise to tell your*

prospect how he can get what he wants if he'll just listen to you.
Let me give you a few examples here to illustrate that idea:

> I'm going to show you how you can get rid of that tired feeling. I'm going to tell you how you can add another full productive hour to your day by getting rid of your fatigue. (Sounds like a vitamin or health food company advertisement, doesn't it?)
>
> I'm going to show you how you can double your present income. (A variety of salesmen use this one, but it's a special favorite of the correspondence schools.)
>
> I promise to show you how you can be more beautiful, be more attractive, and have more sex appeal. All I want is just ten minutes of your time. (This is an old favorite of the door to door cosmetic and beauty aids sales person.)
>
> Let me show you how you can be proud of your floors. (Ever hear a floor wax commercial like that? I'm sure you have.)

In other words, tell your listener immediately what you're going to do for him. Tell him that you're going to show him how to be loved—how to win money or fame or power—and how to stay healthy, the easiest way possible. Do that, and you'll not only have his immediate attention—you won't be able to get rid of him!

This same approach can be used in a talk by putting your information into a challenging opening question or statement like this:

1. "How'd you like to increase production by 25 per cent, improve employee morale, yet save money on your electricity bill all at the same time?" (Salesman for fluorescent light fixtures talking to the production superintendent in a tire and rubber plant.)
2. "You're gambling $10,000 against $50 when you don't want to increase the fire insurance coverage on your house. The odds are 200 to one against you! Even Las Vegas and Reno

give you a better shake than that!" (Insurance salesman trying
to increase the hazard coverage on a man's home.)
3. "Will those two boys of yours get to go to college if something
   happens to you?" (Life insurance salesman talking to a young
   father.)
4. "You can get rid of that messy garbage can forever, Mrs. Jones.
   (Salesman for the In-Sinkerator Garbage Disposal Company.)
5. "Mr. Jones, you lose a quarter every time you sell a pair of
   socks not made by us." (Manufacturer's representative for a
   hosiery firm throws a quarter down on the desk as he says
   this.)

If you'll analyze each one of these sentences for yourself, I
know you'll be able to determine the benefits that are being
offered and the fears that are being counteracted in them. This
kind of opening can also be used to good advantage in your
writing, especially in your sales letters. In how-to magazine articles and how-to non-fiction book writing, it's a nice-to-have,
but in speaking, it's an absolute must.

Now that you've got immediate attention, your next job is to
hold it. Here are some ways you can do just that:

DON'T TAKE MORE TIME THAN YOUR
SUBJECT IS WORTH

"I don't think I've ever seen a church before where people
stood in line to get inside," I said to Dr. Raymond Vance. Dr.
Vance is the pastor of the First United Methodist Church in
Phoenix, Arizona. "What's your secret?"

Dr. Vance smiled broadly at my question, and said, "It's a
secret I learned from my father and it's simply this: *I always
quit before I'm through!*

"You see, my father was always extremely critical of ministers
who kept on preaching after their sermon was finished, especially if they went beyond high noon. He loved to fish on week-

ends, and had he had his own way, he'd have been sitting on the river bank early Sunday morning. However, to keep peace in the family, he took us all to church, and waited until Sunday afternoon to pursue his first love.

"One particular Sunday on the way home from church, my mother asked how he enjoyed the sermon. It was the wrong day to ask. The minister had been unusually wound up, the sermon had run to nearly half-past twelve, and my father was going to be late getting down to the river.

"But with a patience with which I've never been blessed, he turned to her, and said, 'He said more than he had to talk about.'"

This can happen to you, too, if you don't stick to your subject. So the first thing you ought to do is to keep your own goal in mind. What is it that you want to get done? Do you want to sell a washing machine, persuade the boss to install a new piece of machinery, or convince your wife that you need a new set of golf clubs? If you keep whatever you want in mind, you'll be more apt not to digress, but to move quickly and steadily toward your final objective.

This is not to say that you should disregard questions or bulldoze your way over objections. You should, however, stick to your point. As soon as you've answered a question or overcome an objection, get yourself right back on target. Don't wander off course and start talking about the weather or politics or tell him about the latest joke you heard the other day.

"Too many sales can be lost because salesmen talk too much," says Sherman Wilson, an agency manager for the Metropolitan Life Insurance Company. "Once you've closed your sale, stop talking. Get his money or his signature or whatever you're after, and then, to put it quite bluntly—*shut up*. Otherwise you're liable to unsell your sale!"

A simple rule to use, along that same line, not only for selling, but also for putting across any proposition to someone, is this:

1. Get in.

2. Get what you want.
3. Get out.

DON'T TALK TOO MUCH

Stick to the format I've given you of *benefits—techniques—summary* if you want to hold your listener's attention. Otherwise, you're liable to come down sick with the writer's deadly disease known as *manuscript elephantiasis*. Speakers and salesmen are often troubled with the same disease, but their ailment might more properly be diagnosed as *foot-in-mouth disease*. However, the symptoms are almost always the same.

Two of the main causes of manuscript elephantiasis or foot-in-mouth disease are simply lack of self-control in sticking to your original plan and plain wordiness—the love of hearing your own voice or of reading your own writing.

Often your original plan for your sales talk or your sales letter, your speech, magazine article, or book will be a good one, but in your actual presentation you go off on tangents to your main purpose. You digress and wander aimlessly from one point to another, drifting along with complete loss of purpose. Your listener's attention will drift along aimlessly the same way.

The remedy is quite simple. It is merely to come back to your original outline, in this case *benefits—techniques—summary*, and to stick to it. I know of no better one, or I'd be using it.

Wordiness is even more difficult for most people to correct for it's an American custom to use more of everything than we actually need. Most of us think that the bigger the better, and quantity is equated with quality. This definitely does not hold true in writing or speaking.

Wordiness is often called *logorrhea*. It can cause confusion and misunderstanding and complete loss of attention. It is axiomatic that *attention is always lost when understanding is gone*.

To keep the full attention of your listener or your reader, don't talk too much. Make every word count. A sentence should not have any unnecessary words nor should a paragraph have any unnecessary sentences. This is not to say that you must make every single sentence short, or that you should treat your subject only in outline and not go into detail. It is to say, however, that you should make every word tell.

POINTS TO REMEMBER

Just to show you how important I consider this chapter, and also to show you that I really do believe what I say about summarizing things, let me wrap up this chapter for you like this:

HOW TO GET IMMEDIATE ATTENTION— AND HOLD IT

1. Plan your opening statement.
   a. Know who your listener is.
   b. Find out what he's interested in.
   c. Know what you have to offer.
2. Make up an outline.
3. Use this format:
   a. Benefits.
   b. Techniques.
   c. Summary.
4. Don't take more time than your subject is worth.
5. Don't talk too much.

7

How to Lead and Control Small and Medium-Sized Groups

ONE OF THE MOST EFFECTIVE METHODS YOU CAN USE TO lead and control small and medium-sized groups is to teach them how to do their jobs. Yet this method is often overlooked or neglected by many people simply because they don't understand it or know how to use it.

But showing a person what to do—teaching him how to do it—is one of the best ways for you to hold his complete attention, control his actions, and get him to do what you want him to do. In fact, the best leaders have always used principles of instruction to get the job done.

For instance, I personally know that army officers spend 75 to 80 per cent of their time teaching the art of soldiering to their men. Sales managers devote most of their working hours to teaching their salesmen how to improve their sales techniques so they can increase their sales.

General foremen and production supervisors use the majority of their work day to instruct new employees how to do the job and to show old employees how to do it better. And what about safety directors, boy scout leaders, Red Cross first aid instructors, preachers, Sunday school teachers? They all spend a lot of their time in teaching others.

And as business and industry and technology become more and more complex, there'll be an increasing demand for people

111

who know how to teach their skills and knowledge and know-how to others.

True enough, most of the time you'll probably use informal and impromptu methods right on the spot to correct mistakes and get the job done. But how do you handle the training of employee rescue squads so they'll be ready to save a co-worker if there's an accident? Or how do you take care of the training of emergency fire teams—how do you train each man in his individual duties?

And what about the times when more modern machinery is installed, different production techniques are introduced, new sales and management procedures are put into practice? Who's going to take care of all the training and instruction that's going to be needed in each one of those occasions?

You see, sooner or later, the time will come when you'll wish you knew how to teach some group for it'll be the best way you can lead and control them. If you can do it, you'll benefit, for you'll be noticed and remembered as a person who can do much more than just his own individual job.

Just for instance, now, suppose your boss were to call you in some morning and say, "I'd like you to give next month's safety lecture to all our employees. Use a one hour period. You'll probably need to give it at least a dozen times to catch all three shifts and to cover every department. Think you can handle it, or should I get someone else?"

What's going to happen if you say "No"? Oh, there's probably no requirement laid down by your boss that says you have to know how to teach people as well as be a sharp administrator or salesman or accountant or computer programmer or whatever. But what will he think of your abilities to get the job done if you tell him you can't manage it? What will he say?

Or what if you say "Yes" because you're afraid to refuse, knowing full well you're not really qualified to do the job, and you end up making a complete mess out of it?

Either way, if you're not big enough to handle it, maybe he'll figure that you're not big enough to be promoted either. So let me ask you this one question right now: *Will your boss remember you for what you can do—or what you cannot do?*

If you do want him to remember you for what you can do, then keep right on reading. After you finish this chapter, you won't have to say "No" to him. You can say "Yes" with complete confidence in your abilities to do the job. Your benefits will increase and your reputation will spread when you know how to lead and control small and medium-sized groups by using the principles of teaching. Let me show you now exactly how you can do just that.

USE THE SEVEN BASIC GUIDELINES OF GOOD INSTRUCTION

You can use these seven basic principles or guidelines of good instruction to create the most favorable learning atmosphere. These guidelines are motivation, objective, response, reinforcement, realism, background, and incidental learning.

Motivation

Your listener must want to learn before you can teach him anything. To get him in the right frame of mind, to develop the desire in him to learn, you can use one or more of these eight specific motivational techniques so he'll pay close attention to your presentation.

Show Him the Need to Learn. Don't assume that your listener will recognize the full importance of what he is learning just because you do. Much important information may seem completely unrelated to his work when he first hears it. Your instruction should include logical reasons for learning and a full explanation of how he can use the information you're giving him.

"Safety lectures can be extremely boring to most employees for two reasons," says Max Abbott, Safety Director for Hoerner

Paper Products, Inc., in St. Paul, Minnesota. "First of all, the lecture itself is often dull and uninteresting because the instructor simply views it as a necessary evil. Second, the average employee always thinks: *Oh, it'll never happen to me.*

"But some of the machinery in our plant can take off a man's arm or leg in less than five seconds. And I've seen toes chopped off simply because a man forgot to wear his safety shoes with the steel-capped toes one day; or fingers lost when a girl neglected to put on her steel finger guards.

"I have three people—two men and a woman—who help me give the initial plant safety lecture to all our new employees. They really drive home the point of remembering to use proper safety precautions, for they're living examples of people who didn't. Lee's right arm is off at the elbow—Jerry has only a stump for a left foot—and Myrtle has three fingers gone from her right hand."

Develop an Intent to Learn.   Before you give instruction, make sure your listeners understand they are as responsible for learning as you are for teaching. It's not enough that they just be physically present; they must also be mentally prepared to learn. Check their progress often and insist that each person apply himself. An individual always learns more when he's made to realize that he's fully responsible for his own learning.

Maintain Interest.   Interest of your listeners is essential if you're going to gain their attention—and hold it. Your use of personal force, enthusiasm, concrete examples, vivid illustrations, and benefits to be gained will help keep their interest high. The more interesting you make the material for them, the more readily will they learn it.

Just keep in mind, however, that your responsibility is to teach them—not just to entertain them. This is one mistake the amateur almost always makes. He interprets laughter as a sign that his listeners are absorbing the material and that they're getting everything there is to get out of his instruction.

This is simply not so. I'm not cutting down the value of a good joke, if it's related to the subject and helps to get your point across, but if it doesn't do that, then you'd be better off to leave it out.

Encourage Early Success.   Early success always motivates people. A person's success will drive him on to further effort and additional successes, for nothing ever succeeds like success.

For the average person, achievement brings a certain amount of pleasure, satisfaction, and stimulation toward even greater activity. So it's highly important, especially during the early phases of any training program, that you have people work at a project they can complete successfully.

Give Recognition and Credit.   Recognition for achievement and credit for results obtained always provide strong incentives for learning. People want credit for a job well done, and they have a right to expect such recognition. So emphasize the good points; don't linger over their mistakes. Always lead off with favorable comments before you ever go on to make suggestions for improvement.

Never Embarrass Another Person.   Never belittle or criticize another person, especially in front of the group and when they are doing their best to learn. Avoid hurt feelings and emotional responses that interfere with efficient learning. Feelings do affect the rate of learning. People who are angry, resentful, embarrassed, frightened, or otherwise emotionally upset will think about their problems—not about the subject being taught.

Use Friendly Competition.   Friendly competition always stimulates learning, especially if it's team competition. Competition between groups can achieve progress for all as long as you don't allow their competition to obscure their learning goals. Group competition is usually more preferable than individual competition with each other. Having a person compete against his own past record also provides worth-while competition.

Use Reward and Punishment.   Rewards are powerful incentives for learning. On the other hand, punishment is the least desirable method of motivation. In most cases, it should be used only as a last resort.

The imposition of punishment for failure to learn can be thought to be unjust or unfair or too severe by your listener. This can breed antagonism and resentment and end in his failure to learn simply because he now associates the subject with the punishment, so the subject material itself now becomes undesirable.

Objective

The second basic guideline to use in your instruction is that of the *objective*. Remember where you're going, why you're going there, and be sure to let your listener know, too. Learning is always quicker and more lasting when your listener knows exactly what you want him to learn, precisely what you expect from him, and when you expect it.

"The objective in our first echelon preventive maintenance courses is to reduce our maintenance costs and to keep our equipment from being deadlined because of operator carelessness, ignorance, or inefficiency," says Keith Barrick, Maintenance Director for the Central Division of Pacific Gas and Electric. "We want to reduce our operating costs; that's our main objective.

"However, that's much too broad a goal to give to the individual equipment operator in the classroom. So in the actual preventive maintenance classes, our instructors state the lesson objectives in terms of what we want our operators to be able to do, the conditions under which they should be able to do the job, and the performance standards we expect them to achieve.

"People always learn best when they have clearly defined and specific goals. If we want our employees to memorize a definite procedure or to be able to do a specific job or perform a certain operation, we tell them exactly what we want and why we want it, but always in their terms."

Keeping in mind what Mr. Barrick said, you should always tell your listeners at the beginning of each period of instruction the specific goals you expect them to attain. Tell them exactly what they should be able to do and how well they should be able to do it as a result of your instruction.

Not only that. You should also tell them how each lesson fits into the overall program and how the entire course of instruction will prepare them to do a better job.

Response

A person completely learns only that which he does or responds to. If you're teaching him how to drive a car, he'll never really learn how until he gets behind the wheel himself.

His participation can take many forms. He may listen, watch, take notes, recite, or solve problems for you. The instructional process, presentation—application—evaluation, depends upon your ability to use this guideline of instruction so you can get the best response from him.

Plan every period of instruction in such a way that your listener will always have to participate in some manner. Practice makes perfect only when the person himself practices it.

Reinforcement of Response

If you want your listeners to learn more rapidly and to absorb the information better, let them know immediately whether their response is right or wrong. Don't leave them in the dark and make them wonder.

When a person knows at once that his response is right or successful, it will strengthen and reinforce that response and fix it solidly in his mind. He should also be told at once when he is wrong so he can correct his mistake immediately before the error is fixed in his mind.

Ideally, your listener should be able to determine whether he is right or wrong immediately after each response. The longer the delay between the response and the knowledge of the results, the weaker the reinforcement of that response becomes. For this reason, most industrial training and instruction courses depend primarily on a performance type test.

Plan your class so evaluation of your listener's performance will be concurrent with the presentation and application stages of instruction. Immediate on-the-spot correction of errors helps to speed up learning.

Realism

Always relate your instruction to the actual situation as closely as possible. Each lesson or even the main points of each lesson should be tested for realism by these questions:

Is This the Way the Material Will Be Used in Actual Practice?   Material presented in a class should be realistic from the standpoint of its actual application. However, during the introductory phases of instruction, don't allow your desire for realism to obscure learning.

"Just because our linemen may at times have to climb poles in the midst of a blinding snowstorm doesn't mean they have to learn how under such conditions," says Clifford Cole, line supervisor for the Southwestern Bell Telephone Company in Joplin, Missouri.

"We introduce such realistic obstacles as bad weather or darkness into our practical work after our men have mastered basic principles and techniques of pole climbing and line repair."

Is My Presentation Realistic for the Level of Everyone? If your instruction is beyond the comprehension of your listeners, it is not realistic. However, you can present relatively difficult material if you will relate it to your listener's specific needs.

For instance, to make your instruction seem more realistic to your listener, use personal references like these: "Here's what this means to you." "You can use it in this way."

Background

Learning is based on experience. New experiences are interpreted on the basis of past experiences. To properly use a person's background to help him learn, always move from the rule to the exception—from the familiar to the new.

For instance, you can explain many new things by using illustrations drawn from the past experiences of your listeners by relating their past experiences to the new material. For example, resistance to the flow of electrical current through various wire gauges can be likened to the resistance of the flow of water through different diameters of pipes.

You can also use this principle of instruction by referring to information you've given to them previously. This has now become a part of their background and should be familiar to them.

Incidental or Concurrent Learning

When you teach a person how to perform preventive maintenace on a company vehicle, you are also teaching him cost-consciousness and supply economy.

If you're conducting a class for would-be supervisors, remember that your listeners will learn as much from what you are as they do from the material that you're presenting.

That is to say that you must also set a good example for them to follow. You must be enthusiastic and positive about your subject. Say for instance, you're teaching principles of leadership to up-and-coming young supervisors or junior management people. You'll need to know and practice basic leadership principles yourself and to exhibit favorable characteristics of leadership as well as give out technical information.

Now that you have the basic guidelines or the principles of instruction in mind that you can use to lead and control small and medium-sized groups, let's get on to the actual mechanics of it.

STAGES OF INSTRUCTION

Stage	Activities and Methods
PREPARATION	1. Make an estimate of the situation. 2. Select and organize subject matter. 3. Write your lesson plan. 4. Rehearse your plan. 5. Make your final checks.
PRESENTATION	1. Lecture 2. Conference 3. Demonstration

APPLICATION	1. Individual performance
	  a. Instructor controlled
	  b. Independent
	  c. Coach and pupil
	2. Team performance
	  a. Individual phase
	  b. Team phase

EXAMINATION	1. Oral tests 2. Written tests 3. Performance tests 4. Observation
REVIEW AND/OR CRITIQUE	1. Sum up and clarify the lesson. 2. Reemphasize the important points. 3. Correct errors made during application and examination stages. ·

In the stages of instruction, the lesson plan always seems to give most people the greatest difficulty. Just remember it is a blueprint of your planned instructional activities. It is the means to an end—not an end in itself. It should include a checklist of administrative matters, an indication of instructor and student activities and responsibilities, and an outline of main points of the subject matter to be covered.

Above all, keep it simple. It's your lesson plan for your own use. Don't complicate it for yourself. Here's a simple sample lesson plan you can adapt to any subject you might have to teach, no matter what it is:

LESSON PLAN

Heading *

Instructional Unit	(What is the subject to be presented?)
Type of Instruction	(Which method will be used? I.e., lecture, conference, evaluation, practical exercise, or combination.)
Time Allotted	(How much time is available?)
Classes Presented to	(Who will receive the instruction?)
Tools, Equipment, Materials	(What items will the instructor need to supply to the students?)
Personnel	(What instructors are needed?)
Training Aids	(What training aids will be needed? Detailed description of aids can be put in an annex to the lesson plan.)
References	(Where is the subject matter to be found?)
Study Assignments	(What should the student study before class?)

---

* NOTE: Place all information regarding preparation necessary for the conduct of the lesson in the heading of the lesson plan. Do not leave out any elements of the heading. If they do not apply, write *None*. The heading serves as a checklist for the preparation stage.

| Dress and Equipment | (What should the student wear or what should he bring to class?) |
| Transportation Requirements | (What form of transportation, if any, will be needed to transport students to the training site?) |

Body

1. Introduction

(Indicate method to be used and time required.)

NOTE: If some special technique is used to gain the attention of the class, such as a demonstration or a skit, put it into the lesson plan as a NOTE.

a. *Objective.* List the specific things the students are to learn.

b. *Reasons.* Tell why students are to learn the subject.

c. *Review.* Indicate tie-in with previous instruction.

d. *Procedure.* Indicate the instructional activities that will take place during the lesson.

NOTE: The objective and reasons should be included in all lessons. The review and procedure may be used where appropriate. These elements of the introduction may be outlined in any order that seems best for your presentation.

2. Explanation and/or Demonstration

(Indicate method and time needed.)

a. All main subject matter points of the explanation and/or demonstration should be listed and designated a, b, c, d, etc.

b. Supporting points for main subject matter points of a, b, c, d should be listed and shown as (1), (2), (3), etc.

c. When notes, training aids, questions, and other instructional procedures are used, put them into the lesson plan in their correct places like this: NOTE: Show Slide Number 7. Hold up Picture Number 8. Diagram the circuit on the blackboard.

3. Application

(Indicate method and time needed.)

    a. *Directions to Students:*
      (1) Purpose.
      (2) Tools and equipment to be used.
      (3) Procedure for the conduct of practical work.
      (4) Safety precautions to be observed.
    b. *Directions to Assistant Instructors:*
      (1) How to introduce the practical work.
      (2) How to conduct the practical work.
      (3) Checks to be made on presence and working condition of all tools and equipment.
      (4) Supervision of students and assistant instructors.
      (5) Other duties of assistant instructors.
      (6) Summarize the practical work
    c. *Practical Work:*
      (1) Description of the practical work.
      (2) List of problems and answers.
      (3) Practical exercise situations and requirements are normally included as an annex to the lesson plan.

4. Examination
(Indicate method to be used and time required.)
    a. *Written Tests.* Include complete text with directions in an annex to the lesson plan.
    b. *Oral Tests.* Include questions to be asked.
    c. *Observation of Student Work.*
      (1) List specific points to be checked.
      (2) Indicate how to rate or score the students.

5. Review
(Indicate method to be used and time required.)
    a. *Clarification of Points of Difficulty.* Ask students if they have any problem or any questions.
    b. *Summarize the Lesson.*
      (1) List the main points.
      (2) List the key ideas of the main points.
    c. *Make Your Closing Statement.* (Outline in detail or write out.)

Annexes: (If annexes are used to supplement your lesson plan, list them on the last page of the lesson plan, following your closing statement.)

HINTS ON CLASS MANAGEMENT AND CONTROL

A few years ago, the Zenith Radio Corporation established a branch plant in Springfield, Missouri. They did not want to import outside labor into the local labor market so they took it upon themselves to train more than four thousand men and women in the detailed intricacies of assembling and building their world famous handcrafted Zenith television sets.

I was fortunate enough to pick up some hints on class management and control from their Director of Training, David Davenport. I asked Dave if he'd pass those same hints along to you. He agreed to do so, and here they are:

"Before your class begins, there are a few details you should check out first," Dave says. "It can save you a lot of headaches and embarrassment. Check on your seating arrangement—be sure you have enough chairs. No one should be left standing. Check on your lighting, ventilation, instructional materials, equipment, training aids, and assistant instructors.

"When you begin your class, tell your students the nature and the purpose of your instruction. Indicate why it's important to them; tell them exactly what's expected from them. While you're actually instructing, use these seven points to control your class:

"1. Present the instruction forcefully and enthusiastically.
"2. Be alert to class reactions and maintain discipline.
"3. Direct your questions to inattentive students.
"4. Question students frequently to check their understanding and to keep the class alert. Recognize correct answers; correct wrong ones.
"5. Don't let your students waste class time arguing a point.
"6. Handle problem cases by individual instruction.
"7. Illustrate important points with visual aids and examples."

HOW TO ASK STUDENT QUESTIONS

In Chapter 5, I showed you how to use questions to gain information, to change a person's position, sway his way of thinking, or get him to make a firm commitment. You might think, with all that, it would be impossible to discuss the techniques of questioning any further. However, there is a specific way to ask student questions. Here's what it is:

Student questions should—

1. Have a clear purpose.
2. Be clear and concise.
3. Emphasize one point only.
4. Require a definite answer.
5. Be phrased to discourage guessing.
6. Be related to the "how" and "why."

This is the proper procedure to use when asking students a question:

1. Ask the question.
2. Pause briefly.
3. Then call on the individual student by name.
4. Recognize and evaluate the student's response.

HOW TO CONDUCT PRACTICAL WORK

Vocational and technical schools stress on the job training and emphasize the importance of practical work more than do ordinary high schools.

One of the most modern and progressive vocational and technical high schools I've ever seen is Southern Nevada Vo-Tech High School in Las Vegas, Nevada.

One of their instructors in the advanced electronics department, Clarence Woo, gave me an 18 point guide for conducting practical work when I visited the school last fall. Since no doubt most of your instruction will include practical work, I've included it here for you.

HOW TO CONDUCT PRACTICAL WORK

1. Give detailed directions to your students.
2. Be sure they know the "how" and the "why" of it.
3. Inform students as to the standards you expect them to meet.
4. Allow enough time to attain the standards you've set.
5. Stress instruction first—production second in the beginning.
6. Supervise closely and constantly.
7. See that people perform correctly.
8. Learn each step before progressing to the next.
9. Reteach and redemonstrate when necessary.
10. Stress both speed and accuracy after the procedure is learned.
11. Make the application realistic.
12. Ask pertinent questions during the practical work.
13. Be patient and encourage them in their work.
14. See that all safety precautions are observed.
15. Show positive interest in student progress.
16. Have good students aid slower students.
17. Help students evaluate their own performance.
18. Rotate students from one job to another.

I asked my son-in-law, Arch Spain, since he's a school teacher, to review this chapter for me and give me his honest opinion.

"Well, of course, I know you can't begin to tell a person in one short chapter how to be a professional teacher," Arch says. "If you could do that, then I wasted four years in college! But for what you're doing—showing the average person how to lead and control small and medium-sized groups by using the principles of instruction—you've covered the major important points.

"You've given the seven basic guidelines of good instruction; that's important. You also put in the main ways you can motivate a person to learn; that's also a must. I see you also included a section on how to ask student questions. Most people don't know how to do that. And the section on how to conduct practical work is extremely useful. I think most people in business and industry who teach as an additional duty or a sideline would probably use that method most of the time.

"I was much impressed by your lesson plan outline. I've never seen one so detailed and complete. To tell the truth, I'm going to incorporate it into my own teaching methods.

"However, I'd like to add one idea to your chapter and it's this:

> A good instructor will keep it simple—have but one main object—stay on course—remain cheerful—be enthusiastic—put it out as if the ideas were as interesting and as novel to him as they are to his audience."

Now it's seldom that I let my son-in-law have the last word, but this time—I did.

8

Use These Professional Secrets to Put Yourself Across with People

$\mathcal{T}$HE SUCCESSFUL PEOPLE FROM WHOM I GATHERED THESE notes are real pros in the art of putting themselves across with people. Their professions, occupations, and avocations include such diverse fields as professional platform speakers, politicians, television and radio personalities, sales managers, ministers, college professors, high school teachers, football and basketball coaches, boy and girl scout leaders, and many others.

This chapter offers several major benefits that you can gain. First of all, you won't need to make any mistakes; these people have made them all for you and have already got them out of the way. You'll also have the opportunity to learn how to put the finishing touches on your own techniques. You'll have the chance to polish and refine your own style. In fact, you can learn how to become a professional yourself in this fine art of putting yourself across with people.

For instance, you'll learn five ways to control your nervousness when speaking to people. You'll be shown seven ways of getting into your subject without any hesitancy or fumbling around trying to find the handle. You'll learn six tips to use for an effective delivery. From a negative viewpoint, or what *not* to do, you'll find seven distracting mannerisms to avoid and six don'ts to remember that will be of special value to you.

Now then. Let's get right into the subject so you can learn

these professional techniques of putting yourself across with others. Let's start back at the beginning with. . . .

HOW TO CONTROL YOUR NERVOUSNESS

Almost everyone experiences nervousness when he stands up in front of a group to talk no matter how good he is or how long he's been at it. Good athletes are always honed to a fine edge before a game or a fight. Red Skelton, one of the finest comedians in the business, says he still sweats and shakes before every single performance.

So don't think that something's wrong with you if your stomach turns to jelly the next time you get up in front of a group of people to say something. Nervousness simply shows that the adrenalin is flowing and that you're anxious to do a good job. It means you're concerned about your listener's reaction and the reception you're going to get.

People who don't get a few butterflies in their stomach are usually stolid unimaginative persons who do a poor job of putting themselves across with others. As Paul Barnes, a Missouri State Senator, says, "I do not think any speaker is fit to face an audience unless he feels a quickening of the pulse."

When properly controlled, your nervousness will result in a more enthusiastic and expressive delivery. The best way to control your nervousness is to make it work for you instead of letting it work against you.

Bill Glasgow, one of the Keedick Lecture Bureau's busiest and most popular speakers, a man always in demand throughout the country, uses five simple techniques to control his nervousness. I asked Bill to tell you about them so you can use them, too.

"Be Thoroughly Prepared," Bill says. "That's always the first thing you should do to overcome your nervousness. You must master your subject thoroughly. You have to know more about your selected field than your audience. When you're the authority on your subject, it's impossible to put you down.

"**Have a Positive Mental Atttitude.**   Understand that nervousness comes from your fear of what people will think about you. To get rid of that fear, keep a positive mental attitude toward people. Look at everyone as your friend.

"Be confident in yourself. Have faith in your own abilities. When you're the master in your own field, nothing on this earth can keep you from being successful. Simply act as if it were impossible to fail.

"**Have Your Initial Remarks Well in Mind,**" Bill goes on to say. "The first few moments are always the most difficult. Get past those and things will go well for you. Know what you're going to say and then say it. Have your introductory remarks so well in mind that notes of any sort will not be needed.

"**Tell a Story on Yourself.**   Nothing releases tension more quickly or endears you to your audience as a joke on yourself. It must be on yourself—not on someone else—and it should come early in your introduction. It should have a point that is related to your subject. It doesn't have to be a belly-buster. Just a rib-tickler to establish rapport with your audience is enough.

"**Be Deliberate—Slow Down.**   Remember that when you're nervous and overly excited, all your body functions tend to speed up," Bill concludes. "So slow down your movements and make your gestures deliberate. Force yourself to speak more slowly. After only a few moments of such deliberate and precise control, your stage fright will pass away and your normal poise and bearing will come back to you."

SEVEN WAYS OF GETTING INTO YOUR SUBJECT

To establish contact, arouse interest, gain attention, and get into your subject quickly and easily—you can use one or more of the following techniques:

An Effective Opening Statement

Let's say, for instance, you've accepted an invitation to speak at next Thursday's Kiwanis luncheon to a group of business and professional people on the subject of "Community Relations in Industry."

The man who invited you to speak is president of a local manufacturing company with 100 employees—your boss! You know you'll have his full attention at once, and that's for sure.

But besides him, your audience will have bankers, lawyers, doctors, real estate brokers, insurance people, and retail merchants in it. What kind of opening can you use to get everyone's immediate favorable attention? Here's how Walter Parks, Vice-President of Public Relations for Western Electric, says that he would do it:

"First of all, pause for just a few seconds after you're introduced," Walter says. "Remember that you're speaking to a group who've just finished eating and now they're enjoying their coffee and some little private conversations with each other.

"Those few seconds of silence on your part will quiet them down faster than if you were to plunge into your talk immediately. While you're waiting, look over your audience. When you spot a friendly face or see someone looking directly at you, smile at him. You can establish contact with your entire audience by showing your interest in a few people here and there.

"When things are quiet, turn to the person who introduced you and say, 'Thank you, Mr. Smith.' Turn back to your audience and say, 'Good afternoon, ladies and gentlemen.' Then go at once into your talk.

"In a mixed group like Kiwanis, your opening statement must be a *grabber* that will show them immediately how your talk relates to them or how they will benefit by listening to you.

"For instance, most of my talks are titled *Human Relations in Industry, Community Relations in Industry, Industrial*

Peace in the Community, and the like, so I start out this way:

" 'There certainly is no group of business and professional people anywhere more alert to the importance of maintaining good community relations in industry than all of you sitting here.

" 'Even though you may be a doctor, a lawyer, an insurance or real estate broker, a merchant, and may not be a member of industry yourself, you are vitally interested in keeping industrial peace in your community. Industrial peace is beneficial to you and you can exert a tremendous influence toward maintaining it.'

"With those few opening remarks, I've shown my audience how and why my subject is important to them, and how they can benefit by listening to me."

You can do the same thing yourself. Once you've bridged that initial gap between you and your audience with your own *grabber,* your own effective opening statement, then go into the main body of your talk. Develop your major points, always making sure to phrase them in terms of your listeners' interests and benefits.

Make Reference to Some Previous Information

This method is most often used where your contact with your listener is of a recurring nature. It refreshes his memory and reestablishes contact with him on common ground. However, it is not enough just to say, "Last Sunday we talked about . . . yesterday our lesson was . . . the last time we met we discussed. . . ."

You see, even though you're making reference to some previous occasion, you still need an effective opening statement to emphasize a benefit the listener should have gained during that last period of time you're referring to.

For instance, you can say, "In our last meeting, we learned how our product is superior to the XYZ brand in these ways . . . in our last discussion we learned the advantages of family planning . . . the last time we got together we learned the benefits to be gained when. . . ."

Always renew your contact with your listener by talking about a benefit. Always come back to a benefit. Remember that's all the other person is interested in finding out: how he can benefit by listening to you. If you can't tell him, he'll go listen to someone else who can.

Use a Startling Statement

To put yourself across with people at once with a bang, find some eye-opening strong statement that can be used to punch home a benefit immediately.

For instance, if you were a PTA member trying to round up support for a school expansion of some sort, your best bet would be to show people how they could save money in the long run by voting for the project now. That would be to their benefit.

"No one likes to spend money unless he can see some concrete benefit for himself, especially when it comes to increasing school taxes," says Arnold McGrath, president of Glendale High School Parent Teacher Association in Springfield, Missouri. "But if you can show him how he can save money by spending less now than he would in the future, he'll vote for your bill.

"A good example of that was our school parking lot. We needed to expand our student and faculty parking facilities, but the majority of the people were against it until we came up with statistics to show that had we built the parking lot big enough in the beginning it would have cost us less than half of what we would have to spend now, and that if we were to wait another 2 years, the price would go up at least another 25 per cent. The longer we waited, the more money it was going to cost us in the long run. Once we got that point across to people, there was no trouble at all in getting the new parking lot approved."

Dorthea Lubbers, an Iowa distributor for Amway Home Care Products in Webster City, Iowa, says she always uses a startling statement to make a strong and forceful opening when she's telling a potential customer about Amway's washing machine compound.

"I don't believe in wasting time," Dorthea says. "I believe in getting right to the heart of the matter, so I say, 'I don't care what soap powder you're now using, *you're using four times more than you actually need!* You're just throwing good money down the drain. Our Amway washing machine compound, SA-8, can get your clothes cleaner for one-fourth the money you're now spending on your washing machine detergent, no matter what kind it is!' "

Now that's a strong statement, but Dorthea says it's true. Make sure you're telling the truth, too, and be sure you can back up your startling statement with proof and facts when you use one. If you can't, you'll be losing ground instead of putting yourself across with your listener when he asks for that proof from you.

Ask a Question

A question is one of the best ways to open a conversation. Your listener has to respond in some way to you. The moment he does, you've established contact with him.

When I was much, much younger—in fact, I was only 19 and just out of high school—I sold *Ladies' Home Journal* door to door up and down the coast of California from San Diego to San Francisco. I used to carry copies of it under my arm when I went to the door.

I'd hold one copy in my right hand, open the screen door, and ring the bell. When the lady came to the door, I'd hand her the magazine and say, "Here's your *free* copy of the *Ladies' Home Journal.*"

Then I'd turn and start down the walk. After taking just a couple of steps, I'd stop, turn around, and say, "You looked kind of surprised there, Ma'am. You did receive the card telling you all about your free copy and the amazing offer *Ladies' Home Journal* is making, didn't you?"

Well, of course, she'd say "No," simply because she'd never been sent any card. That was only my way of breaking the ice to get the conversation going. So I'd go back and explain the whole proposition to her.

I sold three-year subscriptions to 75 per cent of all those women I talked with. In fact, I'd even get back the *free* copy of the *Ladies' Home Journal* when I left so I could *give* it to the lady next door.

Sure, once in a while, a lady would say "Yes," take the magazine, slam the door, and that was that. After all, I didn't expect to win 'em all. I knew I had to lose a few once in a while. That was just one of the many occupational hazards of selling magazines door to door.

Use an Anecdote, a Story, an Illustration, an Example

People are always more interested in people than in things. If you want to prove a point, there's no better way to do it than to show your listener how it worked for Jim Green, Charlie Grey, or Susie Smith.

Examples of how others benefited by using your methods or your product are more convincing than anything else you can say; no doubt about it.

Take those magazine selling days of mine. I always referred to Mrs. Brown or Mrs. Smith next door or just down the street or around the corner who was now a satisfied customer of mine when I was talking to the next prospect.

People always like to do what other people are doing. No one likes to be first—unless it's a contest—but nobody likes to be left out either. So always use an example or an illustration thats shows how someone else was first and how satisfied they are now.

Always tell your story or give an illustration for a definite and specific purpose. Don't tell a story just for the sake of telling a story. As Jack Kearns, a high school teacher and a close friend of mine, says, "Some persons tell a story just to make conversation and to make people laugh. I'm not being paid to be a comedian. I tell a story to my students to make a point, or I don't tell it."

Quote an Authority

"A testimonial from a satisfied user is still the best way to convince a prospect," says Carl Williams, president of his own Los Angeles advertising agency. "And if that satisfied user is also an authority in some field, or if he's a celebrity and well known to the public, so much the better.

"That's why today you see big time movie stars and TV personalities appearing in so many commercials as well as the John Smiths and the Sally Browns. Every time I turn around there's Arthur Godfrey or Eddie Albert selling me soap again.

"In some commercials where you can't see their faces, you'll often recognize the voice, or at least, you think you do. In a lot of cases, that voice *just happens* to sound exactly like the real personality, because that's exactly what the advertiser wants you to think. A voice that sounds almost like Walter Brennan, Greogry Peck, Dean Martin, or Buddy Ebsen gives that commercial a definite stamp of authority."

Use a Demonstration

Back in the days before refrigerators automatically defrosted themselves, George Biederman made a fortune selling a small electrical gadget for $9.95. This little device was the first automatic defroster. You simply plugged it into the wall plug and then you plugged your refrigerator into it. Then your refrigerator would automatically defrost itself every 24 hours or whatever cycle you set for it.

"To tell the truth, I never sold a single one," George says. "They all sold themselves. I'd simply ask permission to install one for a week with no obligation whatever to the person. At the end of a week when I came back, if she liked it—she paid me for it. If she didn't like it, I simply unplugged it and took it with me. I made no sales talk of any sort. Most women met me at the door with the money in their hands. In five years, I took back a total of nine! That was all. Most times, I couldn't have got it away from a woman even if I'd paid her to get it back!"

Whatever your particular job is, you can use a demonstration to get your point across. When you do, you'll increase your chances of putting yourself across to others. One picture is still worth ten thousand words, no matter how far we've come into this modern technological era.

If your company hasn't given you a pat made-to-order demonstration to use, then dream up one just as I did with *Ladies' Home Journal*. That was all my own idea—not theirs. I can't allow them to take any of the credit.

FIVE TIPS FOR AN EFFECTIVE DELIVERY

"Many salesmen, a lot of teachers, ministers, politicians, foremen, supervisors, and just plain ordinary people end up making speeches and lectures or talking *at* people, but they never really get around to talking *with* them," says Doctor E. Richard Kline, an industrial psychologist with General Motors.

The whole purpose of talking with another person is to get your ideas or your thoughts across to him—to put yourself across with him—to get him to do what you want him to do. If that's not your point in talking with your listener, then there's not much use in doing so.

If you do want to put yourself across with people, you must establish contact with them and keep that contact at all times.

You must stay in control. Doctor Kline says there are five ways you can do that, and I've asked him to cover them for you in detail.

"Get His Attention First," Doctor Kline says. "Don't start your actual pitch until you have the other person's full attention. You don't need some fancy trick gimmick to get a person to listen. Many times, the simplest way is still the best way. Just ask him to listen to you. Promise him a benefit for doing so. Simply say, 'I have something interesting I'd like to tell you that will be of *great benefit* to you.' This statement will produce the result you want 95 per cent of the time.

"Look at Your Listener When You Talk with Him. This is extremely important for an effective delivery. You can't establish rapport with your listener unless you look him straight in the eye.

"A good speaker may not realize he is looking his listener in the eye. It may be automatic with him. If you don't have that natural knack, don't worry about it. You can develop it. Simply address your listener—not the floor, the ceiling, the window, or some part of the landscape.

"Start out by looking at his forehead. Then move slowly down to his eyes. Give every person the feeling you're looking directly at him and speaking only with him. Keep eyeball to eyeball contact with him at all times.

"Speak in a Conversational Tone," Doctor Kline goes on to say. "You don't have to orate or declaim even if you're speaking to a large group to put yourself across with others. You can still keep a conversational tone to your voice.

"You can give the impression of carrying on a personal conversation even if you're giving a speech or a talk to a group by the frequent use of the pronoun *you.* Identify yourself and your listeners by *you and I* or *we.* This gives the definite impression that you and your listeners have something in common.

"Show a Definite Interest in Your Listener. Although your main purpose in speaking with John Jones may be to serve your own interests, that point should never come to the surface to

be seen. You must show John how he can benefit when he accepts your proposition. You see, John's interested only in himself and if you want to put yourself across with him and get what you're going after, you'd better learn to take a deep interest in him and in what he wants. It's the best way to keep him on your hook.

"Be Alert! Look Alert!" Doctor Kline says in conclusion. "Know what's going through your listener's mind. Pay close attention to his face, his remarks, his responses. Listen carefully and evaluate his comment and his answers to your questions.

"Learn to read between the lines so you can pinpoint the reason behind his questions and his answers. And remember this, too, if you will. It's just as important, sometimes much more so, to *listen to what he didn't say* as much as to what he did say.

"Be quick to spot the slightest loss of attention on his part. Continually ask yourself, 'Does he understand me? Am I getting through to him?' Check frequently with questions to be sure he does understand you and that he's following what you're saying."

MAINTAIN A PROPER BEARING

Although Doctor Kline listed five tips for a more effective delivery, there is also a sixth one he did not mention that is important. That one is to be sure you maintain the proper bearing.

You see, people respond to what they see as well as to what they hear. In putting yourself across with others, you must maintain certain standards of appearance, posture, and body control.

Your movements and your gestures can be highly expressive and extremely influential in helping you to make your point. They can make the difference between an excellent enthusiastic presentation and a dull and lifeless one.

Any physical attitude you assume, any body movement, or any

gesture that attracts attention to itself rather than helping your efforts is distracting to your listener. It then becomes a hindrance rather than an aid to you. To be helpful, your movements should be free and spontaneous. Remember to be as natural as you can be at all times.

"To maintain a proper bearing in front of your class or in front of your listeners, you should do these three things," says Robert Johnson, a speech professor with Drury College.

"*Maintain an Erect Posture*," Mr. Johnson says. "Take a position where your entire group can see you. Stand erect with your weight evenly balanced on both feet. Don't slouch. You don't have to stand rigidly at attention as if you were in the army, but you should look physically and mentally alert. The key to an erect posture is to *think tall*.

"*Be Enthusiastic*. There is no substitute for a physically vital and enthusiastic delivery," Mr. Johnson goes on to say. "Enthusiasm is contagious. If you're sold on your subject, your audience will know it; you don't have to tell them so. As a result, they'll be interested and anxious to learn. Of course, the whole basis for a person's enthusiasm is a thorough knowledge of his subject and an understanding of how it can benefit his listener.

"*Use Gestures, Too*," Mr. Johnson says in conclusion. "It's amazing to me how many speakers don't use gestures to get their point across, especially teachers. I suppose college professors think they're too dignified to do so.

"But you can use gestures to convey a thought or an emotion, to emphasize your point, or to reinforce your words. I always try to make mine as natural as possible. I never rehearse them.

"When you use gestures, they should come spontaneously from your enthusiasm, your convictions, your emotions. Don't try to emphasize every sentence with a gesture. If you did that, you'd look more like a windmill than a good speaker, and only defeat your purpose."

SEVEN DISTRACTING MANNERISMS TO AVOID

Along that same line, and while Mr. Johnson's comments about bearing are still fresh in your mind, I'd like to have Reverend Virgil Springer, a Presbyterian minister, tell you about several distracting mannerisms to avoid, whether you're a teacher, a salesman, a minister, or a housewife addressing the monthly meeting of your PTA, your weekly Sunday school class, or a Red Cross fund drive. Here's what he has to say:

"Five of these I learned in the seminary," says Doctor Springer. "The last two I added during my service as a chaplain in the army. The first one you should look out for is—

"*The Dying Warrior.* In this position, the speaker leans heavily on his lectern. He wears an air of total exhaustion and never moves. All he needs to complete this picture is a feather drooping down over his forehead from an Indian headband.

"*The Fig Leaf* is favored by the speaker who has no lectern to lean on. In this position, he stands solidly with both hands clasped in front below the waist, feet eighteen inches apart and completely immovable, his body solid as a statute.

"*The Walkie-Talkie* is a descriptive term in itself, too. This person is the pacer who never stands still for a single moment. I think most *Walkie-Talkies* are frustrated would-be lawyers who imagine themselves walking back and forth in front of the jury box.

"*The Chained Elephant* stands first with his weight on one foot—then on the other. He goes nowhere, but constantly moves his feet in position—just shuffling back and forth.

"*The Change Counter* constantly counts the change in his pocket every two minutes or so. Or he runs a stream of half dollars or quarters from one hand to the other constantly.

"*The Swordsman* is one I picked up in the service. As a military chaplain I gave character guidance lectures where I used charts and a pointer. I soon found I had picked up the bad habit of fighting imaginary duels with my pointer. I was constantly stabbing at everything within reach even when I wasn't actually using it. The only way I could get rid of the habit was to hang the pointer up on its hook on the chart stand when I wasn't using it.

"*The Baton Twirler* is more advanced in his techniques than is *The Swordsman*. He uses his pointer as if he were entertaining the crowd at half time. This requires a lot of skill and dexterity. That's why I never picked up this bad habit."

SIX DON'TS TO REMEMBER

Senator John Morrisey from Indiana gave me these *Six Don'ts To Remember*. He says he considers them as fundamental techniques for the politician to use. I'll say they're good for a lot of other people besides politicians, too. Here's what they are:

"*Don't Bluff*. Never bluff to cover up a lack of knowledge," Senator Morrisey says. "No matter whether you're a salesman or a teacher, a foreman or a supervisor, a doctor, a lawyer, or a politician, you should know your subject thoroughly.

"Even so, no matter how knowledgeable you are, questions will come up that you can't answer on the spur of the moment. Things are too complicated today for you to be a walking dictionary. If you don't know the answer, say so. Find out what it is and let the person know as soon as you can.

"*Don't Use Profanity or Obscenity*. Not even a tiny 'Damn!' is permissible. Look at what happened to the astronauts on the Apollo Eleven mission. The moment you use profanity, you run the risk of losing your dignity and respect and the attention of your listeners.

"*Don't Use Sarcasm or Ridicule*," Senator Morrisey goes on to say. "This is especially true if you have a captive audience. School teachers, military officers, employers, senators, in fact, anyone in authority is likely to violate this principle. And your listeners will become resentful of you when they can't respond in the same sarcastic manner. When a person resents you, you'll never put yourself or your point across with him.

"Don't Talk Down to Your Listener. You might be much smarter than your listener—but only in one subject and you selected that one. So there's no reason to treat him as an ignoramus or a dummy. You should consider yourself fortunate to have had the chance to gain your knowledge and experience. Now you ought to be willing to share it with others.

"Don't Lose Patience. If your listener asks you to cover a point again, don't get upset about it. His inability to understand you could very well be your inability to explain it clearly. You'll simply have to repeat the information or switch to other methods and techniques to explain your point.

"Don't Make Excuses. This is my last don't," says Senator Morrisey. "Ever sit in an audience and hear the instructor or the Sunday school teacher or the main speaker say, 'Ill prepared as I am to speak . . . I didn't have a chance to go over this material . . . I'm really not at all qualified to talk on this subject . . . I wouldn't be up here, but they couldn't get anyone else. . . .'?

"Sort of leaves you cold, doesn't it? Well, the other person feels exactly the same way if you tell him things like that. Don't apologize or make excuses. Never make any remark that could be interpreted as an excuse for lack of preparation, lack of knowledge, inability to speak, and the like. Excuses only accent your weaknesses."

And there you have it: some of the secrets of the professionals themselves. Use them yourself and you'll improve your delivery and sharpen your style. You'll increase your ability to put yourself across with people.

Now let's get on to another subject that's just as important to you: how to use special techniques and special procedures to put yourself across.

9

How to Use Visual Aids
to Get Your Point Across

*A*LL TOO OFTEN, WE DEPEND ON WORDS ALONE TO CON-
vey our meaning to our listeners. We *tell* when we could do a
much better job if we would *show*.

We give a complex and detailed oral presentation with many
facts to consider and then depend on our listeners to recall
those points without the help of written supplementary material.

We often fail to make use of visual aids in our communication with others. A good mixture of oral and visual techniques
often provides the solution when misunderstandings occur or
when problems of communication appear.

A good drawing, for instance, will often do the job in less
time with less effort and better effect than will a well-planned
one hour lecture. A pencil sketch at just the right moment in
the conversation will help you communicate an idea or a con-
cept that would be virtually impossible to put across with words
alone.

For instance, imagine that you have a friend who's never
seen a football game before. You're trying to explain it to him
by using only words. You're not allowed to draw him a picture
or a sketch of any sort. You can't even use gestures. Now it
would be almost impossible for him to figure out what you're
talking about. But just let him watch a game on TV while

you're explaining it to him, and even before it's half time, he'll have its basic rudiments quite well in mind.

Visual aids can be a vital part of your presentation, too. *You can use them as a powerful tool to help put yourself across with people.* Besides that one big benefit, here are three more you can gain when you use visual aids.

VISUAL AIDS HELP HOLD YOUR LISTENER'S INTEREST

Visual aids add interest and vitality to your communication. They help focus your listener's attention on the point that you're making. When properly used, they lend variety and spice to your presentation.

VISUAL AIDS PROMOTE BETTER UNDERSTANDING

One of the most important reasons for using visual aids is to make it easier for your listener to understand you. Good aids simplify your presentation, add emphasis and punch, and help to clarify difficult points. Your listener will more easily understand you when he can physically see what you're talking about.

VISUAL AIDS ARE TIME-SAVERS FOR YOU

Visual aids help your listener learn more rapidly. You can then use the time you've saved to do other things or to tell your proposition to more people. And time is always valuable. It's truly your greatest asset in life. The older you get, the more you'll realize that. I already have.

Now let me tell you how the rest of this chapter is set up: First of all, I'm going to cover briefly some of the more *common visual aids you can use* and go over a few of their main features with you. Then I'll give you some *characteristics of a good visual aid*. After that, I'll go into the *techniques of using visual aids,* followed by a few *precautions* to keep in mind. And I'll finish up this chapter by showing you how to go beyond visual aids so you can *appeal to the rest of a person's five physical senses* so you can put yourself and your proposition across to your listener.

KINDS OF VISUAL AIDS YOU CAN USE

There are a variety of visual aids that you can use. Each one has certain advantages and disadvantages. Your choice will be largely influenced by size, complexity, cost, time, purpose, and availability.

Actual Equipment.   The actual equipment is the most realistic visual aid you can use. However, you must consider the size of your group when using the actual equipment. Your listeners should be arranged so that all can see.

For instance, it would be extremely hard to get 10 to 15 dental students situated so they could all look into one patient's mouth at the same time. Or if you were showing some of your people how to assemble and disassemble a new piece of machinery in your plant or how to operate it, you might run into the same problem.

If you were teaching apprentice mechanics how to adjust a carburetor, time an engine, or remove spark plugs, use of the automobile engine itself as a visual aid could make it extremely difficult for all of them to see.

If you do encounter problems like these, you should supplement your presentation by using other visual aids in addition to the actual equipment. One of the best ways to do this is to suspend a large mirror over the actual work so that your entire group can see what you are doing. When the mirror is tilted properly, any number of people can sit comfortably and watch the entire procedure. This kind of visual aid is most often used during surgery in university hospitals so that medical students and interns can watch the actual operation on the patient.

Models.   Models are frequently used along with or in place of the actual equipment. They are recognizable three-dimensional representations of the real item and are usually built to scale.

Mockups.   Mockups are imitations of the real thing. They may, but do not have to be similar in appearance. Some elements of a mockup may be eliminated to focus your listener's attention on others.

Graphic Aids.   Graphic aids can include charts, diagrams, graphs, sketches, cartoons, maps, and the like. The proper use of color can add to the effectiveness of graphic aids. For example, the color red could be used to emphasize the electrical system of a vehicle engine, the color green to identify the fuel system, and the color yellow to show the hydraulic system. Color should be used primarily for emphasis.

Venetian Blinds.   This visual aid looks much like an ordinary venetian window blind. However, the venetian blind strips are mounted individually in a wooden frame resembling a box type picture frame. The overall size of the frame—height, depth, and width—depends on the number of venetian blind strips you want to mount.

The venetian blind is a very effective visual aid to outline main points. The lettering on a venetian blind strip should be neat, attractive, and orderly. Capital letters large enough for all to see and read should be used. The items should be uncovered one at a time and discussed thoroughly before the next item is exposed.

Venetian blind strips should be summarized in the order in which they are presented. In other words, start from the top and summarize from the top.

Chalkboard.   The chalkboard is a flexible and extremely useful as well as economical visual aid. The chalkboard is more commonly known as the *blackboard* to most people, but that term is a misnomer, since the chalkboard does not have to be black. Green chalkboards have become much more popular since they do much to overcome glare and eye fatigue.

Green chalkboards can be easily and cheaply made by painting a hard smooth piece of plywood with a flat green oil paint. Yellow chalk will stand out clearly on this kind of board. Not only that, more colors of chalk can be used on green chalkboards than on black chalkboards.

Films, Film Strips, and 35 MM Slides. The preparation of professional films and film strips for use as visual aids goes beyond the abilities of the average individual. This is a highly specialized field and far beyond the scope of this chapter.

However, this is not true of 35 mm slides. You can do a good job with them. I have used slides with good results in many of my lectures.

The Opaque Projector. Although somewhat cumbersome and bulky to handle and carry around, the opaque projector can be used quite effectively to project material directly from textbooks, magazines, newspapers, and other printed materials on a wall or screen. All features that are highlighted in color or special print will appear on the screen the same way.

I would like to point out that although I have experimented with every single one of these visual aids, I have always come back to charts. I have found them to be the least expensive and the most practical visual aid for me to use with my lectures. It could well be that you'll find the same thing to be true.

CHARACTERISTICS OF A GOOD VISUAL AID

Under this heading, when I talk about the characteristics of a good visual aid, I'm not referring to the actual equipment. This section is primarily to show you how to develop your own ideas.

Then you can come up with your own visual aid that will help you put yourself and your proposition across with people. Before you can do that, however, you ought to know the basic characteristics of a good visual aid so you can come up with your own.

A Good Visual Aid Should Be Appropriate

Any visual aid you use should be relevant to your subject. It should help you clarify a point, stress a feature, or point out a benefit to be gained by your listener. In planning your aid, consider the size of your group, the place where it will be used, and the distance from the rearmost individual.

Make sure your aid can be seen by everyone. If it cannot, you'd be better off without it. If you're using charts, for instance, the lettering should be no less than two inches for every 32 feet from your aid. And that's the minimum. Since most of us don't have perfect vision, the bigger the letters—the better.

A Good Visual Aid Will Be Simple

Your visual aid should be simple and easy to understand. If a child in the eighth grade cannot understand it, then chances are it's too complicated for the average listener. Visual aids, just like the words you use, should be kept at the eighth grade level of comprehension or below to be most effective.

Not only that, unnecessarily complicated aids can cause your listener to focus his attention on your aid rather than on your proposition. The best way to keep your visual aid simple is to get rid of all unnecessary information and details that don't help you get your point across.

Your Visual Aid Should Be Accurate

Be sure your facts and figures are right. Telling the truth is just as important here as it is when you're talking about your actual product or service. Don't let your credibility be destroyed by a misleading visual aid.

Your Aid Ought to Be Portable and Durable

Although some aids are permanent and never move—for example, the climbing poles in an area used for training telephone linemen or the parachute jumping towers in Fort Benning, Georgia—in most instances it's best to keep your aids compact and portable.

They should be light in weight or constructed into easily assembled parts to insure easy movement. Don't end up with a boat in the basement. If your aid is moved a lot, it should be made from durable materials that hold up well under rough handling.

Your Aid Should Be Easy to Use

Your visual aid ought to be easy to work and operate. Intricate and complicated devices might be of value sometimes, but normally speaking, the most effective aid will be simple, neat, and practical.

A good visual aid should be designed to help you make your point or illustrate your idea without interrupting the continuity of your presentation. It should also be constructed so it can be shown to your listener without distracting his attention from what you are saying.

Your Visual Aid Should Be Attractive

Your aid should be attractive to your listener. Dirty and grimy visual aids turn your listener off immediately. If you're using charts and some of the pages are smudged from excessive handling, then have them made over.

Neat clear lettering and correct spacing will add eye appeal and make important points stand out. Too many words will clutter up your aid. Whatever you do, don't end up with a visual aid that looks like this:

THiNK AHEAD!

Use Color and Movement

Two things always attract a child: color and movement. The most successful toy manufacturers always consider these two points first when they're thinking up new ideas for their products.

The *Hula Hoop* is the classic example of a simple toy that used only these two points to make it successful and the manufacturer supplied only one of them: the color. The customer had to supply the movement himself.

Color, used wisely, will help you to emphasize your main points. Again, caution is in order, for too much color can become distracting to your audience.

Movement can also be used to call attention to major features. However, a word of warning is in order here, too. In short, if a part moves, it should have a reason to move. Don't create movement solely for the sake of having movement. You run the risk of ending up with a Rube Goldberg if you do that.

Your Visual Aid Should Be Necessary

Each visual aid should illustrate essential material and help you achieve your goals. It should be the means to an end, not the end in itself. I've actually seen salesmen and teachers, supervisors and managers become so engrossed in their visual aids that they completely lost sight of the real purpose behind them.

Above all, don't use visual aids merely for eyewash, to kill time, or to entertain your listeners. Visual aids, just like jokes, should not be used if they do not help move you toward your final objective.

HOW TO USE VISUAL AIDS

Professor Norman Haines teaches an adult education course at Park College in Kansas City, Missouri, in the use of visual aids. Hundreds of businessmen, executives, management people, salesmen, and teachers attend his classes.

He attracts all kinds of people. In fact, the last time I sat in as an auditor on one of his lectures, the man sitting on my right was a young Baptist minister. The girl on my left was a social worker. I've asked Professor Haines, since he's such a recognized expert in the audio-visual field, to give you the correct techniques for using visual aids.

"Prepare in Advance Drawings or Data that Consume Time," Doctor Haines says. "A chalkboard, more commonly known as a blackboard to many people, is a wonderful aid, but when a mathematics teacher spends half his class time writing on it instead of teaching his students, it loses its value completely.

"You'd be much better off to make up flip charts if you have to move from one part of a mathematical formula to another. The more time you spend in preparing your aid in front of your listeners, the less time you'll have to explain and the less attention you'll receive when you finally have it ready. In fact, if you don't have a captive audience, some of your listeners could've already left you!

"Prepare Yourself in Advance for Using Your Aid. Know your visual aids thoroughly so you can answer any questions about them. Rehearse your presentation several times to your-

self using the aid exactly as it will be used later on in the live performance.

"If you're using flip charts, for example, you can write in your outline the title of the next chart so you can make reference to it before you turn to it. This procedure helps you smooth out the transition from one point to another and also makes you look as if you really knew your stuff cold.

"I learned that technique from my minister years ago. I used to marvel at the way he could move swiftly from one reference to another in his Bible during his sermon. I would have sworn he knew the entire Bible by heart.

"He would start off by reading some scripture. Then he would say, 'And in Matthew 5:44 we find . . .' Then he would turn to that scripture. After reading it, he would say, 'We also find confirmation of this same fact in Luke 6:27.' And he would then turn to that scripture. And so it went.

"One day I asked him how he could retain such a tremendous number of scripture references in his memory, know the material each one contained, and be able to cross-reference the way he did.

"He smiled and then gave me his secret. 'I know the first reference,' he said. 'I have to know that, but it's the only one I know. Let's say the subject of my sermon is *Love Your Neighbor as Yourself*. I want to establish a scriptural basis for my theme so I'll start with Matthew 19:19, for example, where it says, 'Thou shalt love thy neighbor as thyself.'

" 'Now on that page I will have a tiny card inserted there that says, *Turn to Mark 12:31 on page 39*. Inserted there will be still another card that says, *Turn to Romans 13:9 on page 124*. Each one of these references, of course, will have to do with loving your neighbor as yourself. And that's how it's done.'

"You can do the same yourself. It makes you look like an expert and gives you instantaneous knowledge and wisdom.

"*Introduce Your Aid at the Proper Time*," Doctor Haines goes on to say. "The best way to do this is simply to keep your aid covered or out of sight until you're ready to use it. Large charts can be hidden by covering them with the same blank paper you used to make your charts from.

"Or if your chart has lines of printing, you can cover them with strips of paper that can be removed one at a time. However, in this case, I would recommend the use of a venetian blind style of visual aid. Machinery, models, and mockups can be covered with cloth much as a painter would cover your furniture when he paints.

"*Explain Your Visual Aid.* Elaborate aids are often used to illustrate highly complicated and technical subjects. When you first show this kind of aid, briefly explain its purpose or its function. Otherwise, your listeners will try to figure out its purpose themselves and miss part of your presentation.

"*Show the Aids So All Can See.* Display your visual aid so that all your listeners can see it. If your aid is a chart or a graphic portfolio, view it from the back of the room yourself to make sure it can be read. Don't guess or take someone else's word for it. If necessary, change the seating arrangement so all can see. The best visual aid in the world is of no value whatever if everyone cannot see it.

"*Talk to Your Listeners—Not to Your Aids,*" says Doctor Haines. "Don't get so involved with your visual aid that you forget your audience. And along that same line, don't stand in front of your aid so that some of your listeners cannot see it.

"Even if you're disassembling a piece of equipment, you should maintain visual contact with your listeners. When you're explaining a chart or a drawing, stand along side of it. This will help you get rid of any tendency to talk to the aid instead of your listeners.

"*Use a Pointer.* A pointer is extremely useful to focus your listeners' attention on a particular part of your visual aid. Hold it steadily on that part of your aid that you want your observers to notice. Always hold the pointer in the hand nearest the aid so you can keep better eye-to-eye contact with them.

"If you hold the pointer across your body, you tend to talk

to the aid rather than to your audience. *And always put the pointer away when you're not using it.* It's easy to pick up distracting mannerisms with a pointer when you're not using it.

"Use an Assistant to Your Best Advantage. If you're using someone to help you, say a clerk or your secretary, make sure they are well-rehearsed, too. They should know exactly what they are to do and when they are supposed to do it. If your assistant is going to show 35 mm slides for you, for instance, you should have a prearranged signal so he will know when to change slides or when to turn off the projector.

"Display Your Aids Smoothly," says Doctor Haines in conclusion. "If you're using several visual aids, number them in the order in which they're to be used. If heavy equipment has to be moved in and out, make sure it can be done quietly without unnecessary disturbance. It could well be that in some instances you'd be better off to take your audience to the aid rather than bringing your aid to the audience."

SOME PRECAUTIONS TO BE OBSERVED

Carefully check over your product or your service so you can figure out when, where, and how you can use visual aids to help put your point across to your listener. To help you out, let me say you should always keep this one specific idea in mind whenever you're planning to use a visual aid of some sort:

Never fit your proposition to your visual aid.
Always fit your visual aid to your proposition.

If you don't keep this idea in mind, you will suddenly find your listener is more interested in your visual aid than he is in your actual proposition! If your visual aid doesn't help put your product or your service across to your listener, then it's of no value to you whatever. It's only a novelty and should be discarded.

Also, keep in mind that too many visual aids will not get the job done for you, either. Again, quantity is no sign of quality. Too many aids will only create confusion and can keep your listener from understanding your proposition.

Along that same line of thinking, don't use visual aids for *eyewash.* Keep them up-to-date. If your chart covers only through the first quarter of the fiscal year and you're now in the third quarter, don't make excuses for not having the latest figures posted. "I haven't had the time" is never an acceptable excuse to anyone.

GOING BEYOND VISUAL AIDS; APPEALING TO ALL FIVE PHYSICAL SENSES

Most people use only words—the sense of sound—to put themselves and their message across to others. Thinking individuals will go further than that and use visual aids to help put their point across.

But the really farsighted person—the imaginary and creative person—will not only use sight and sound to make his point, but he will also *smell, touch,* and *taste* if at all possible.

You see, learning and understanding take place with the stimulation of one or more of these five senses. And the more of them you stimulate, the more likely it is that permanent learning and understanding, and therefore—acceptance of your proposition—will take place.

So use your imagination; be creative. You'll be able to reach your listener and put yourself across with him through every sensory channel. Let me show you specifically what I mean by this:

Take a Woman, for Instance.   A woman is a walking illustration of what I'm talking about. She knows better than any other living creature how to use her built-in aids and put herself across with a man by appealing to all five of his physical senses —*sight, sound, smell, touch, taste.*

You see a beautiful woman across a room at a party and you are attracted by the *sight* of her. She comes closer and speaks softly to you. You are thrilled by the *sound* of her voice. She lays her hand on your arm and your skin almost burns from the *touch*. Your interest in her deepens. You *smell* an implied invitation in the provocative perfume she's wearing. You brush her cheek fleetingly with your lips and that quick *taste* of her sends your imagination soaring in fantasy.

People in the advertising business know full well the importance of appealing to as many of the person's five physical senses as possible. And so do some extremely farsighted and highly creative and imaginative business men and women. Let me give you some concrete examples to show you exactly what I mean.

How to Do It if You're in the Food Business

Many restaurants, steak houses, and sandwich shops have found they can increase their business by cooking right out in front of the customer. This way they can appeal to more of a person's physical senses than they could if he were to order his meal from a dead-looking menu and never get a chance to see what he's going to eat before it arrives at his table.

Take yourself, for instance. You go into a restaurant. You're starving for a big juicy steak The waitress brings you a menu. You might have wanted the biggest steak in the house when you came through the door, but when you look at those prices, you settle for the cheapest rib steak you can get. *Whenever you read a menu, the price always becomes of primary importance.*

Now let's change the situation completely. Instead of ordering from a menu, you go to a restaurant where you can actually *see, smell,* and *hear* your steak cooking. That restaurant has appealed to three of your five physical senses rather than just one.

And you supply the other two—*touch* and *taste*—in your imagination as you stand there watching those steaks sizzle. So now, instead of ordering the cheapest steak on the menu, you'll be a lot more likely to go for a top sirloin, a thick T-Bone, or a choice porterhouse.

The Bonanza Sirloin Pit, a franchise operation, has become a top favorite with many people all over the country because the entire cooking process is all right out in plain view.

A famous steak house in Portland, Oregon, *The Golden Steer,* goes even further than that. They give you a bite from their "tasting steaks" to help you reach your decision. Then they let you pick the porterhouse, T-Bone, sirloin, or New York cut that you want right out of the display case before it ever goes on the charcoal broiler. I ask you now: Who'd ever be able to order a thin rib steak after tasting a choice porterhouse or New York cut?

A coffee shop, *The Doughnut Hole,* in Newark, New Jersey, uses an exhaust fan to blow the aroma of freshly ground coffee beans and hot doughnuts down on the persons passing by the front of their place. Can you imagine what happens when hungry people walk by, especially on a cold and wintery day in January or February? They've enlarged the place three times and still there's standing room only.

Jimmy Wong, owner of Wong's Tea House in Torrance, California, says, "Half the enjoyment of eating Chinese food comes from using your sense of smell!"

How Other Businesses Use the Sense of Smell, Too

The sense of smell, which is a natural for bakeries and restaurants to use, has long been neglected by many businessmen and advertisers as a major method to promote and sell their products. But the sense of smell can play a major part in separating your customer from more of his dollars.

For instance, Hale's, a sporting goods store in Waterloo, Iowa, increased its sales of fishing gear and camping equipment 20 per cent simply by following my suggestion of putting a fresh pine tree scent into its air circulating system.

Sales to *men* in the ladies lingerie department went up over

30 per cent in Farrahs, a variety store in Des Moines, Iowa, when the management sprinkled suggestive perfumes along the counters and the display cases as I'd suggested.

George Frank, owner of Frank's Men's Shop, an ultra-exclusive store in Dallas, Texas, told me that the sales of expensive men's toiletries nearly doubled when he placed open bottles of various shaving lotions and body colognes on the counter for people to sample. Amazingly enough, most of their increased sales were to women who were evidently interested in making their men even more masculine.

"The average person doesn't realize there's so much profit in popcorn," says Howard Garth, a movie theater owner in Memphis, Tennessee. "Popcorn sales actually kept many a movie from going under back in the thirties. Back then I learned to blow the smell of fresh popcorn into the air ducts.

"I still do that today. I don't have to take a 15 minute refreshment break right in the middle of the main feature and irritate people. By blowing the smell of fresh popcorn in front of their noses every 15 minutes or so, I keep a constant stream of customers going to and from the concession stand."

Bannister's Shoe Store in Topeka, Kansas, put my idea of using the sense of smell to promote customer attention and interest into practice and increased their sales 15 per cent. All they did was use a small fan to blow the clean sharp smell of fresh shoe polish into the air in front of their store.

Nate Shukert, owner of Shukert Furriers in Minneapolis, Minnesota, says, "If two mink coats are modeled for a male customer and one model is wearing a seductive and sexy perfume while the other girl is not, he'll almost always buy the mink the perfumed girl is wearing. Naturally, that one is always a couple of hundred dollars more than the other one!"

Remember Charlie Ryan, the Kenmore washing machine salesman you met back there in the beginning? Well, Charlie also uses the sense of smell to turn his prospects into customers. He puts a few drops of Clorox into the wash water of the model he's demonstrating. It makes his listener feel that the Kenmore can get her clothes cleaner simply because it smells that way!

And that just about sums this chapter up. I do know that you'll be able to get your point across a lot better to your listener if you'll at least use visual aids rather than depend on words alone.

I'll also bet that you can do even a better job if you'll just turn your creative imagination loose and concentrate on stimulating *all* your listener's physical senses instead of depending only on his sense of sight and sound alone.

10

How to Handle Special Occasions
and Special People

THIS CHAPTER IS SORT OF A POTPOURRI OF BENEFITS YOU
can gain. It will show you how to talk and act in a meeting from
two viewpoints: one, that of being a participant; two, that of
being the chairman. It will also show you how to talk at employees' affairs. A most interesting and highly beneficial section
tells you how the experts give a VIP briefing. And the final
section gives you some tips on how to build good community
contacts for yourself.

HOW TO TALK AND ACT IN A MEETING

How you talk and act in a meeting will depend a great deal
on whether you're holding the meeting or attending it. So first
let me give you some pointers on what to do when you're invited to attend a meeting. Then I'll give you some tips on how
to handle one when you're in charge.

What to Do if You're Attending a Meeting

Be Prepared. Some meetings are routine, for instance, weekly
sales and supervisory meetings or staff conferences. Even so,
it's still a wise idea to drop by the office of your boss's secretary

the day before and find out if anything special is going to be taken up this week.

This is a healthy procedure to follow, even for routine weekly meetings, so you can always be ready to answer your boss's questions. But if he's called a special meeting for some reason, then it's a must for you to find out what's on the agenda.

And speaking of special meetings with the boss, *especially if you're the only person invited,* I've learned something else during my long years of experience with people that holds true 95 per cent of the time.

If the boss calls and says he'd like to get together with you this afternoon *in your office*—no problem; don't worry about it. Very few people have ever gotten the ax in their own office. A boss likes to be sitting behind his own desk when he has to take punitive action. That desk is his symbol of authority.

But if he call you and tells you to be *in his office* at two PM sharp this afternoon, then you'd better think twice and really find out what's going on. The roof may be just about ready to cave in on you.

My point is that *where that meeting is being held* with your boss can be a major clue as to just how important it is.

Be on Time. I know of no other single thing that can so easily make you appear to be careless, negligent, and inefficient to your boss than being late to his meetings.

That might be the only time he sees you during the week, so you want to be sure you make a good impression on him. Being on time is an easy way to do that and to put yourself across with him.

But if you're always late, he'll start wondering if you run your own department or section in the same slipshod manner. He's bound to have some doubts about you and your operation; he just can't help himself.

A small point, perhaps, but it can become a mighty big one in your boss's eye. If you want to be known as a reliable person who can be depended on to get the job done, then always be on time.

Don't Ask Questions that Waste Other People's Time. If you have a question that's going to affect most of the people in the meeting, then ask it by all means. If it's a question that could change current policies and procedures for everyone, then every person there should know the answer, of course.

But if your boss's answer is going to affect only your operations, then it would be far better to take it up with him after the meeting on an individual basis. Most employers leave an opportunity at the end of a meeting so that individual problems can be solved without wasting everyone else's time.

Contribute What You Can to Make the Meeting a Success. It could be that you don't like to attend meetings any more than I do. When I was in the army years ago, I used to wonder how the regimental commander ever expected us to get any work done, for we were constantly being called to attend one of his innumerable staff meetings!

Maybe you feel that way sometimes, too, but if you're a junior executive or a valued employee in the company, you'll need to cooperate with your boss for your own benefit, so you might as well do it willingly and cheerfully.

"One of the best ways to show your willingness to cooperate with your boss is to contribute your ideas and opinions *when they are called for,*" says Wayne Ingram, Director of Industrial Relations for Southern Electric Manufacturing Company in Jacksonville, Florida.

"The person who takes the lead in offering *practical* suggestions and *logical* solutions to problems at a staff conference will be looked upon by the boss as a dependable and valuable associate: the right kind of person to have around when the going gets tough.

"If you're that kind of person, you'll soon be marked for promotion. You'll be given a helping hand up the ladder without a doubt, for your opinions and your ideas will come to be respected. Just make sure your contributions are sensible and worthwhile."

If You Don't Understand, Say So. Don't be afraid to ask a

question if you don't understand. If you're confused about a
point, then chances are someone else is, too. They're just afraid
to admit it. Your boss won't look at you as a dunce for asking
a legitimate question. You'd be better off to ask for clarification
so you can do the job right than not to ask and end up doing
it wrong.

What to Do If You're in Charge of the Meeting

Introduce New People. This not only makes for good fellow-
ship, but it also makes it easier for people to get together without any inhibitions. If a lot of people attend your meetings, it
would be a wise idea to have them wear a slip of paper with
their name on it pinned to the breast pocket of their coat or
shirt.

The only really sensible thing I recall about the army was its
policy of having everyone wear name tags. This simple procedure saved all of us a lot of embarrassment when we couldn't
remember someone's name.

Have Your Exhibits Ready. If you have exhibits to show,
make sure they're ready. If you're using charts, make certain
that an easel or an A frame is available and that your charts will
turn easily. Nothing can be more disgusting during a meeting
than to have some of your exhibits missing, out of order, or
stuck together.

Start Your Meeting on Time. Just because you're the boss,
that doesn't mean you should have any special privileges on this
point. If you personally are paying your employees, I'm sure
you won't want them just sitting idly on their hands waiting for
you. They can't make money for you that way.

And if you're not paying them, but you're a supervisor, a
manager, or an executive of some sort in a corporation, that's
still no excuse for being late. I don't care how high you go in
your organization, someone will still be keeping tabs on you,
too.

"If a Record Should Be Kept, Appoint Someone to Do So,"
says Rex Jarrett, city manager of Monterey, California. "Nor-

mally speaking, if a meeting is worth holding, then it ought to be worth keeping track of.

"Have your secretary record the minutes of your meeting or use a tape recorder to do so. Show when and where it was held, who was present, what was discussed, and what decisions were made.

"After your meeting is over, have the notes typed up, okay them for reproduction, and send mimeographed or Xeroxed copies *within 24 hours* to all people who attended your meeting. This procedure will keep them from making mistakes because of some point not completely understood during your meeting."

Don't Take Up Personal Matters with Individuals. If you want to take up a sales problem with your sales manager, don't waste your warehouse foreman's time unless it's going to affect his operation. Every section or department will have unique problems not common to all. It's best to handle those with the concerned parties on an individual basis.

Summarize the High Lights. Before you close your meeting, it's best to again emphasize the major points you discussed. The basic format for your meetings should be: Tell 'em what you're going to tell 'em; tell 'em; tell 'em what you've told 'em!

Don't Hold a Meeting Unless It's Necessary. This is another one of my pet peeves at the army. I've attended all kinds of weekly staff conferences where nothing new was discussed. Why was the meeting held then? Out of pure habit—nothing else.

So if you want to put yourself across with your own employees, don't hold a meeting just for the sake of holding a meeting. To do that is to use about the same kind of logic a church women's group uses when it meets in order to raise money to meet the budget in order that they might have a place to meet to raise money to meet the budget!

HOW TO TALK AT EMPLOYEES' AFFAIRS

Good employee relations are important in every company. Satisfactory human relations must be established inside before you can ever hope to have good public relations on the outside.

There should be all kinds of opportunities in your company to hold special affairs or celebrations that will be attended by most of the employees. Many times you will be invited to speak. Talks like these should be handled carefully.

Don't look at them as distasteful or time-consuming or unnecessary. You can use these occasions as splendid opportunities to put yourself and your company across with your employees. Everything you can do to promote better employee management relations in your company is an important part of your job.

"Invent Opportunities to Improve Human Relations in Your Company," says Fred Justice, Director of Public Relations for the Springdale Rubber Company, Kansas City, Missouri. "The number of such affairs you have throughout the year will depend entirely on how much you want to make out of it. It's entirely up to you.

"For instance, you could honor certain employees for length of service, using a five year period as a basis. If you honored people for every five years of consecutive service up through 25 years, that would give you at least five different occasions to speak to almost everyone in the company.

"And you don't have to limit such special occasions only to celebration of years of service. You can hold a special function when someone gets married, especially if they both work for you; if someone is celebrating an important anniversary of some sort; returns from service in the armed forces; or performs some especially meritorious feat that is worthy of recognition.

"Whatever the reason for the special occasion, you can make it an affair that gives everyone a chance to get into the act. These events help bring everyone in your organization closer together. They establish a feeling of unity and harmony between you and your employees."

For instance now, along Mr. Justice's line of thinking, here's an outline you can follow for an after-dinner speech to celebrate the safe return of one of your people from the armed forces.

1. Offer him congratulations on a safe return to his family and friends.
2. Mention some significant aspect of his military service—awards, decorations, service medals, promotions, etc.
3. Welcome him back into the company. Let him know how really happy you are to have him back with you.
4. Talk about his previous good services with you. Tell some of his previous contributions to the company.
5. Wish him the best of luck, and express your personal desires for his continued success with your organization.

Now let's look at an outline you can use for celebrating a person's length of service with your company.

1. Extend your own personal congratulations.
2. Feature the fact he has come up through the ranks; mention some of his previous jobs and responsibilities.
3. Recall some of his earlier days with the company.
4. Stress his personal development: character, industry, reliability, resourcefulness, cooperativeness, etc.
5. Tell some well-known aspect of his present work that is worthy of special praise and attention.
6. Mention how the company has benefited from his long years of service.
7. Tell some of the good things his co-workers say about him today.
8. Offer him congratulations on behalf of both the company and the employees.
9. Present him with a suitable gift or service award.
10. Express your personal wishes for many more happy and useful years ahead, no matter whether he's retiring from your company or staying on with you.

Now, just another thought or two about these functions for length of service. During the earlier years, it might be best to honor groups of people and speak in more general terms about all of them at the same time.

But when a faithful employee has attained many years of loyal service, then it would be far wiser to honor him on an individual basis and be more selective in making up your guest list.

I've given you only the two outlines here. However, you can use them as guides to make up your own outlines to fit any other occasion or situation. And they can easily be lengthened or shortened to suit your own individual purposes and the amount of time you have that you can use.

HOW TO GIVE A VIP (VERY IMPORTANT PERSON) BRIEFING

It used to be that only heads of state, high ranking government officials, generals, admirals, presidents of corporations, and chairmen of boards of directors rated VIP briefings.

However, today, because of the enormous volume of technical information and statistical reports he has to cope with merely to keep up with current developments, the average corporation executive, plant manager, and businessman all have to depend on briefings by their subordinates—junior executives, foremen, supervisors, department heads—to keep themselves fully informed and up-to-date on the situation.

So no matter how junior you are in the organization, you might as well accept the fact that sooner or later you'll have to give a briefing to someone. VIP briefings are here to stay.

Let me tell you now several things that a VIP briefing is *not* used for. A VIP briefing is not used to persuade or to get a person to take action or make a decision. It is not used to impress or convince your listener of anything. Nor is it meant to entertain him. *A VIP briefing should be used only to inform.* That is all it's meant for; it has no other legitimate purpose.

You can look at a VIP briefing as a way of giving up-to-date information about your own operation to someone who is either your senior or your superior.

GUIDELINES FOR A VIP BRIEFING

Restrict your subject to fit your time

If you've been given only half an hour to talk, and you think you need an hour to tell all about your entire operation, then something has to give—either your time or your subject.

Since the time of your VIP is so limited—that's why he has to resort to briefings in the first place—chances are you'll simply have to condense your talk and *cover only the major points of interest about your operation.*

You'd be far better off to stick to a single point, and cover it well, than to try to cover everything and leave nothing but a blurred and vague impression of confusion in your listener's mind. Later on, though he may not remember your name or your face, he'll think of you as "that fellow who was so confused he really didn't seem to know what was going on in his own department."

Arrange your ideas in a logical sequence

Almost all ideas can be developed logically by using a time or procedure sequence. In the time sequence, for instance, you could treat your subject from the viewpoint of past, present, and future. Or you could begin at a specific date and go forward or backward from there.

"A procedure sequence is especially useful in industrial briefings," says Tom Kelly, production superintendent with Republic Steel. "It begins with the raw material stage and moves through each step of the manufacturing process until the finished product is reached.

"If you were in charge of a production line, for example, you could brief your visitors by starting with the smaller component parts and move down the line to your final assembly point."

Number your points as you make them

One of the best ways to keep your briefing neat and clean and to show you know what you're talking about is to enumerate your principal points of interest. Be specific about doing this; no need at all to be vague and backward about it. Simply say it this way: "My first point is . . . the second thing I want to talk about is . . . third, I want to consider . . . last, I want to say. . . ." You'll be remembered as a person who really knows his business.

Compare the strange with the familiar

Remember when you're briefing someone about your operation, you are the expert—he is not, no matter how many degrees he has or what his position is. What might be quite ordinary and commonplace to you might seem extremely strange and complex to him.

If your field is computers, for example, don't expect the corporation president to be a programmer himself. Always remember that executives work with people—not things. If you're going to tell him how computers work, compare them with something he's familiar with—something he can understand.

Avoid technical terms

Along the same line, don't use purely technical terms. You might be briefing the chairman of the board, but that doesn't mean he understands the exact technical terms of your department.

"I once watched a smart young chemist in the research and development department of a cosmetic firm brief the corporation president," says Donald Larson, an executive with Universal Laboratories in Salt Lake City, Utah. "He wanted to show his listener how much he knew and how important his job was.

"So he used every technical word he could think of to

impress his boss, although he normally translated his highly technical and scientific terminology into ordinary common words for the men who worked in the compound room and on the mixing tanks.

"Unfortunately, the president thought he was trying to make a fool of him, so a week later he summarily fired him. 'If that young man tried to make a fool out of me with his big vocabulary and his college degree, think how much more he'd try to make fools out of the men in the plant,' he said. 'We can't afford to have his smart-alecky kind around. Plenty more chemists where he came from.' "

An unfortunate situation, without a doubt. The thing is, you don't make monkeys out of corporation presidents, whether you mean to or not.

Use audio-visual aids

Even VIPs enjoy audio-visual aids. It's the fastest way of transmitting information and it saves valuable time for them. So use them. Your listeners will appreciate you and your efforts all the more when you do.

Now a VIP briefing is different than any other kind of lecture or talk you'll ever give. Being so unique, it also has some very distinctive pointers or briefing tips to keep in mind.

Don't Summarize a VIP Briefing. A VIP briefing is in a sense a summary in itself. It should be a synopsis or an abridgement of your operation. Your listener assumes that you've included only those major points of interest that he should know. The restatement of those major points is not at all proper and fitting for a briefing audience.

Don't Ask Questions. The idea of using questions to check on audience understanding or for any other purpose is entirely out of place here. Whatever you do, don't insult the intelligence of your listeners.

Don't Emotionalize. Remember the purpose of a VIP briefing. You are not giving a talk to persuade or get action or a decision. You are not trying to impress (at least, you shouldn't be) or convince. Nor are you trying to entertain. *A VIP briefing is used only to inform.* Please remember that. Therefore, you are not allowed to argue for your own ideas. Such an approach would be extremely distasteful, perhaps even embarrassing, to a VIP.

Be Factual. Your briefing must be an unbiased presentation of the facts, and only the facts. No coloring or shading is permitted.

Be Formal. I'm sure this idea will come as a bit of a surprise to you, but remember you're speaking to VIPs. I don't mean your briefing should be stuffy and dull or rigid and inflexible. Nor do I mean you should use 4 and 5 syllable words and automatic verbs with upswept tail fins.

I do mean you should not assume a casual or highly informal attitude. Don't use a sweatshirt and sneakers approach. Your delivery can be natural and relaxed, yet it should be kept businesslike and systematic.

One of the best ways to keep your VIP briefing on a friendly yet completely formal basis is to address every man there as "Sir" and every woman as "Ma'am."

Be Flexible. Thorough preparation and confidence in yourself give you the ability to react quickly to changes in time schedules, to answer searching questions, and to adjust to a variety of different audience attitudes.

Be Brief. Because your listener's time is so valuable, you must be concise in your presentation and in answers to questions.

Don't Use a Strong Closing Statement. Since you are not making a speech to persuade someone to do something, make a decision, and the like, a strong closing statement to get the listener to take action is not in order. The best way to close is simply to say, "Ladies and gentlemen, this concludes my briefing."

HOW TO BUILD GOOD COMMUNITY CONTACTS FOR YOURSELF

Good community relations help build your reputation and spread the word. They can play an important role in helping you build your career. A variety of clubs and organizations are interested in civic and social affairs, education, charity, religion, politics, and business.

You should easily be able to find one that appeals to your own personal interests, and that, through the friendship of its members, will fill your life with satisfaction and contentment.

Smart corporation executives and business leaders look for opportunities to take an active part in the affairs of their communities. And they insist that all their executives and their employees do the same thing.

Even though you're a busy housewife and mother, that doesn't mean you have to be left out. You can always find some interesting activity to join where you can meet people and make new friends.

You might not be able to contribute your efforts on a full-time or permanent basis, but you can always participate in temporary activities such as a church bazaar, a Girl Scout fund drive, a PTA meeting, or a local civic election. These opportunities will give you the chance to build good community contacts for yourself.

And you can be sure that such clubs, drives, and organizations will welcome you with open arms. They're anxious and eager to have your help. Offer your services and you'll find plenty of opportunities for you to get together with local civic leaders who'll appreciate you and respect you for your efforts to help.

You Can Develop Good Will for Your Business

"If you're a businessman, you have an excellent opportunity to develop good public relations and good will for your business when you're working with community groups," says George Latimer, owner of Latimer Hardware Store in Columbus, Georgia.

"Business relations and community relations are dependent upon each other. As you serve your community in one way or another, you will become better known to civic leaders and important people in the town. People always tend to do business with someone who's interested in betterment of his own community."

So spread the good word about yourself by joining clubs and civic organizations in your town. You'll do many things of interest; you'll learn many things of value; you'll acquire a reputation as an individual who gets things done . . . a good person to know and to do business with.

And you'll also find that life will be much more interesting and worthwhile. You won't find yourself bored with life, as so many people are, when you forget yourself and think of others.

Speak Willingly at Community Affairs

Occasions are bound to come along when you'll be asked to say a few words or to make a short speech at some community affair. Whatever you do, don't refuse. This is the chance you've been waiting for. It's a splendid opportunity for you to spread yourself even further and make your ideas and suggestions known on a city-wide or even larger basis.

"Contrary to what many people think, most politicians don't get into politics just because they are lawyers," says Jack Morse, former United States Congressman from Indiana. "They get into politics because they're interested in community affairs in their own home town. They soon learn that if they want to be successful in either politics or community relations, they must know how to talk with people. They must reach the position where their opinions and their ideas can be heard. You don't become a community leader or a politician sitting at home behind closed doors.

"An important point to remember—whether you're on the platform campaigning for office or soliciting money for some charity—is to keep the *we* attitude and the *you* approach. If you start sounding like an individual instead of a member of the group, you're bound to lose a great deal of your group support.

"People always want their community leaders, their congressmen, and their senators to speak *for* them—not *to* them or *about* them. If you talk only as an individual, expressing only your own ideas and your own opinions, they'll soon get the impression that you're interested only in yourself and that you're only using them as a tool to get what you want. They'll feel you're only seeking some personal advantage instead of some benefit for the entire community."

So follow Congressman Morse's advice, even if you're not planning on running for a political office. Talk with people as if you were representing them, as if you were concerned only with their interests, and you'll gain their solid backing and strong support.

Do It from the Heart

When you become interested in community affairs, don't do it with tongue in cheek. You'll be as phony as a three dollar bill. Do it with all your heart. Go all the way; go for broke.

"When you join a club or an organization in your town, don't stop there," says James Neff, President of the Junior Chamber of Commerce, in Fayetteville, Arkansas, home of the famous Razorbacks.

"Become an active member of that group. Take part in everything they do. Don't refuse to serve on a committee. Volunteer to help. Don't be bashful or afraid to join in. Just because you pay your dues or contribute some token service, that doesn't mean you're really community minded. A person is accepted into an organization, not just for the dues he pays, but also for the worthwhile services he can contribute to the entire group."

So think in terms of not what you can get, but what you can give. The more you give, the more you'll get back. That's an irrefutable law of human relations and community affairs.

Giving wholeheartedly is the kind of service that makes you an important member of your community. It builds up your good name and your good reputation. Then you can't help but benefit.

Community service is one of the best ways I know of to learn how to put yourself across with people. So pitch in and do it.

11

How to Put Yourself Across With the People Who Work for You

*W*HEN YOU KNOW HOW TO PUT YOURSELF ACROSS WITH the people who work for you, you'll benefit by having employees, associates, and friends who will—

1. Respect you and have confidence in you.
2. Give you their willing obedience, their loyal cooperation, and their wholehearted support.
3. Work with initiative, ingenuity, and enthusiasm.
4. Work together as a team with high spirit and morale, and with purpose and direction toward a common goal.
5. Feel that they belong where they are.
6. Work just as hard as you do to get the job done.

Now to gain these benefits for yourself, you'll need to know what your employees want most from their jobs and from you, and the amount of importance they attach to each one of those wants.

Luckily for you, you won't have to run your own survey to find out. The American Management Association has already done that for you. They asked more than three thousand employees of business and industry throughout the entire country these two questions:

1. What do you want most from your employers?

2. How would you place those wants in their proper order of importance?

The answers they gave are recorded for you in this chart:

EMPLOYEES' NEEDS AND DESIRES LISTED IN ORDER OF IMPORTANCE BY EMPLOYEES

1. Credit and recognition for the work they do.
2. Interesting and worthwhile work.
3. Fair pay with salary increases.
4. Attention and appreciation.
5. Promotion by merit.
6. Counsel on personal problems.
7. Good physical working conditions.
8. Job security.

Are you surprise at the importance, or the lack of it, placed on some of those points by the employees? You are not alone. The American Management Association also asked the supervisors of those same three thousand employees—their employers, managers, foremen, supervisors—to rate the same items, not in the way they personally felt about them, *but in the order they thought their employees felt about them.* Here, now, are the answers management gave:

EMPLOYEES' NEEDS AND DESIRES LISTED IN ORDER OF IMPORTANCE *BY THEIR EMPLOYERS*

1. Fair pay with salary increases.
2. Job security.
3. Interesting and worthwhile work.
4. Promotion by merit.
5. Attention and appreciation.
6. Good physical working conditions.
7. Credit and recognition for the work they do.
8. Counsel on personal problems.

Now to gain the most value from a survey like this, you should always notice which items are given the most importance and which items are given the least importance. In other words, focus your attention mainly on the top and the bottom. The middle of any survey tends to grow more shadowy, vague, and ill-defined.

For instance, the average man may have a hard time determining whether he should give an item in the middle of a survey a priority of four, five, or six. But that same man has no trouble at all in deciding which items should be one and two, or which items should be last or next to last. He knows those things that are most important to him and those that are least important to him.

As you can see from this survey, employers expected their employees to attach the most significance to pay and job security. But their employees were more concerned about recognition and credit for their efforts, and in having interesting and worthwhile work to do. Job security was the last thing they thought about.

Employers also thought that credit and recognition for the work they did would be one of the least important things to their employees, for they placed it way down the line in position number seven, right next to last place. But to their employees, credit and recognition for their work was most important of all.

So if you want to be able to put yourself across with the people who work for you and get them to do their best for you, to do what you want them to do, you'll need to put your main emphasis on what they want, *not on what you think they ought to want*. Here's how you can do just that:

GIVE HIM CREDIT AND RECOGNITION
FOR THE WORK HE DOES

Let a Person Know He's Both Needed and Wanted.   When a person knows his efforts are appreciated, when he feels he's contributing something worthwhile to the achievement of a common goal, he'll feel that he's actually needed and wanted by you.

You've made him feel important, not only to you, but also to himself. He'll go all out to get the job done for you. He'll be proud of himself, proud of his work, proud of you, and proud of the organization, too.

"No one wants to be a nobody," says Norman Rice, president of Rice & Associates, a San Francisco executive placement service. "Everybody wants to be somebody. No one wants to be just another number, another desk, some faceless or nameless anonymity.

"Everyone wants to retain his own special identity. A person will go to great extremes to be heard and noticed and gain attention, simply because of his fear of being ignored and not listened to.

"The desire to be important and the fear we will not succeed at it is a driving force in all of us. So much so, it often happens that a person will leave an excellent position because he feels his efforts are not being properly appreciated.

"Although he has worked long hours—even though he's done an outstanding job—his superiors have not given him the credit he feels he deserves for his efforts. His need for credit, recognition, and self-importance is given a severe jolt. So he quits and comes to us."

Learn to Say Thanks for a Job Well Done.   It's amazing to see how much sunshine will come into a person's face when you think enough of him and his work to say, "Thanks a million, Sam; well done. I really do appreciate it."

"I am proud of you" are five of the best words you can ever use to make another person feel important and to give him credit and recognition for the work he's done. You can use them any time to praise your employees, your associates, your friends, your husband, wife, or children. They'll always work miracles for you.

"I've never found any better words to use with my Little

League baseball team than *I am proud of you*," says Tim O'Hara, of Rye, New York. "When a boy makes a clean hit or a good throw or a tough put-out, just to say, 'Good job, Bill,' doesn't fetch it.

"But if you nudge his chin gently with your fist, give him some skin, and say, 'I'm proud of you, Bill!'—why, man alive, he'll play his heart out for you."

It'll work for you, too; I guarantee it. In fact, you can use it on everyone, for it works on all—both large and small.

Put It in Writing.   After you say "Thanks," after you tell him today what a good job he's done for you, then tomorrow give him the credit and recognition he wants in writing.

You don't have to send him a formal letter of commendation every time he does something. But you can send him a short note of appreciation. He'll put it in his file of memoirs, maybe even frame it, for written letters of thanks don't come along very often for most of us.

I have for years now used Thank-U-Grams, originated and copyrighted by the Kimball Foundation, to express my appreciation to people in writing. They have matching envelopes and look like the samples on pages 181 and 182.

If you'd like to get some of these to use for yourself, you can order them from the Kimball Foundation, 24 Northcote Drive, Brentwood, Missouri, 63144.

Give Credit When It's Due.   Not only is it important to give credit, but it's also important to give it *when* it's due. Not giving the proper credit when it's time is about the same as sending someone a late birthday card. It never carries quite the same thought as the one that gets there on time, no matter how appealing its message is.

The person who got your late birthday card knows you forgot all about it, and that you don't really care. So does the person who works for you. The man with the birthday also knows you're probably not sending that card now because you really want to; you're doing it only as an afterthought of obligation. Your employee feels the same way.

THANK-U-GRAM

In recognition of the good you have done

181

So if you want to make the most out of giving a person credit and recognition for a job well done, tell him so right away. Don't wait until tomorrow to compliment him for a good piece of work that he's done today. Much of the value will be lost. Tell him now. Timing is fundamental in saying "Thanks." It's a must.

"Add dignity and Stature to His Position," says Byron Underwood, Personnel Director for the Western Engine Company, in Addison, Illinois. "You should always take special care to add dignity and respect to every employee's position, no matter how low and menial it might be. If you think for one single moment that every person doesn't look at himself as the most important person in the world, you're wrong.

"And he looks at his job the same way, too. As far as he's concerned, his job is as indispensable as he is. You might know better, but what will you gain by telling him so?

"That's why today a janitor is no longer a janitor. He's a custodial engineer, or a first echelon maintenance engineer. A street cleaner is, at the very least, a sanitation worker. In most cities, he's a sanitation engineer. A garbage collector is no longer a garbage collector—he's a garbologist.

"Those titles might sound funny to you and me, but the fellow who holds down one of those jobs isn't going to be laughing with us. His job is no joke to him. You can give him the credit and recognition he wants by giving his position an important sounding title, no matter what it is."

Take a Personal Interest in His Job. You can take a personal interest in a man's work by asking him questions about it and by listening courteously to his answers as he explains it to you. Let him tell you how he does it; let him explain the details to you.

Make him the expert. Compliment him on his skill, his know-how, and his abilities. Even if you can do the job better than he can, don't tell him that. Instead, tell him you couldn't begin to do the job nearly as well as he does. I usually believe in telling the truth, but this is one time I'll make an exception. And I hope that you will, too.

Give His Wife and Children a VIP Tour of the Plant. One of the best ways to give your men credit and recognition for what they do on the job is to conduct the wives and children on a plant tour just as if they were VIPs.

This gives your employee a perfect opportunity to let his family know exactly what he does and how vital and important his job is to the company. These tours do take some planning, some forethought, and some work—but they pay much more than they cost.

MAKE HIS WORK INTERESTING
AND WORTHWHILE

Throw down a Challenge. This is one of the best ways you can use to make a person's work interesting and worthwhile. Throw down a challenge, set up certain production standards and then dare your employees to beat your system.

"No one likes to turn down a dare," says Andy Stevens, production superintendent for the Washington Electric Company in Cleveland, Ohio. "When we started our production incentive and profit-sharing plan in the plant, our employees had to use their imagination, initiative, and ingenuity to beat the system, produce more, and earn more incentive pay.

"The more money they make for themselves, the more money they make for the company. This system inspires them to think, to work harder, to want to produce more, to figure out better ways of doing things.

"The incentive system is the best way I know to make a man's work interesting and worthwhile. Even the man who does nothing but put a nut on the end of a bolt can enjoy his job more when he makes a bet with the company as to how many nuts he can put on in a day's time. And that's what the incentive system is all about."

Give Him More Responsibility.   If you have a man who wants more opportunity to succeed, then give him a project of his own and the freedom to do with it as he wants. Just make sure he understands he has full responsibility for its success or failure.

Offer him the chance to make good, and chances are, he'll work like the dickens to make the project go. When he does succeed, he'll increase his own confidence, his self-reliance, and self-respect. Nothing motivates a good employee more than to discover he's better than he thought he was. When he finds that out, you'll also find out that you've gained a more valuable employee.

Emphasize Skill—Not Rules.   No matter how routine his job is, your employee will enjoy it more if he has some way of expressing his own individuality in his work.

I've visited plants where employees were made to stand up when they could've done their jobs just as well sitting down. "Why?" I asked. "Plant rules," was the answer.

My answer to them wasn't quite as short, but at least it was more sensible. "You should learn to rule by work," I said, "not work by rules. Then maybe you wouldn't have to call in a team of efficiency experts to find out why your employees' morale is so low."

If a man can do a better job standing up—he should stand up. If he can do as good a job or better sitting down—he should sit down. The less energy he burns to sustain himself, the more energy he'll have to burn for you.

You should consider only three main factors here: *safety— quality—quantity.* Let your people work in whatever way suits them best, and you'll find they'll stop using their brains to figure out some way to break your rules. Instead, they'll use them to see how they can help you. They'll use their ability, talent, initiative, and ingenuity to help you put out a better product.

Let Him Tell You How and Where He Needs to Improve. As long as you use an incentive system, you won't have to spend a lot of time criticizing the work of your people. They'll be busy criticizing themselves, for the more they produce, the more money they'll make. Low production, both in quantity and quality, is a man's best critic. This is especially true in team operations.

"Much of our work here is done by three and four man units," says Bill Kessler, a department foreman with General Electric's Toledo, Ohio plant. "So there has to be cooperation and team-work.

"If one man is holding up the progress of his team, they'll pitch in and help him do his job. But if he's a deadbeat, they'll get rid of him a lot quicker and easier than we in management can."

You'll probably notice that I've given more time to the first two techniques than I have to the next six. This is not to slight the remaining six techniques, but after all, the first two were the ones those three thousand employees said were most important to them. That's why I've given them the most emphasis.

However, you can't just use the first two and stop. You've got to go all the way, especially since the next one has to do with money. After all, you can't buy bread and butter and beans and bacon with just a pat on the back and an interesting job. It takes money to live, too.

GIVE HIM A DECENT SALARY WITH PERIODIC INCREASES

All of us are interested in money. Talk to your employees in terms of financial reward and you can be sure you're talking about something they understand and that they're deeply interested in. Who doesn't like money, now, I ask you?

Of course, if you pay a person a decent salary to begin with, and if you offer him periodic raises, based on both seniority and skill, you'll be fulfilling one of his basic needs.

But money is a *need* only up to a certain level. After that level is reached, then money becomes a *want*. You cannot dangle the *need* part of a man's pay in front of him like the proverbial carrot in front of the donkey and hope to get what you want from him. He'll simply leave you and go to work somewhere else where he is paid a decent living wage.

However, you can use the *want* part of his salary as an incentive to get a person to really put out for you. Aim for his heart, use what he wants as an incentive, and you'll get results.

I realize that you might be in the position—as so many managers, foremen, and supervisors are—where you cannot control the pay scale of your people. If this is true, then you must bend over backward to increase the benefits they receive in other areas.

"A sergeant's pay is controlled by Congress," says Captain David Patrick, a U. S. Army basic training company commander in Fort Leonard Wood, Missouri. "Since I can't raise his pay, I make every possible effort to give him full credit and recognition for his work and to make his job more interesting and worthwhile. A letter of commendation or appreciation for his efforts and his achievements won't take out all the sting on pay day, but it'll make the pain a lot easier to bear."

GIVE HIM ATTENTION AND APPRECIATION

Not only does a person want you to look at his job as being important, but he also wants you to look at him as being important as a human being, too, separate and distinct from his job. In other words, he wants you to appreciate him as a human being and to treat him as one, rather than as a piece of office furniture or a human extension of the plant machinery.

Remember His Name. One of the best ways to give a man attention and show him that you do appreciate him is to remember his name and use it. People want to be known by their names, not by their clock numbers, or by "Hey you!" or "Fellas."

A man's name is the most important word in all the English language to him. So use it; it'll work magic for you when you do. But if you forget it or mispronounce it, you're asking for trouble.

You should know the first names of your people, you ought to know their backgrounds, and you should have as much information as you can get about their families, too.

What man could help but respect you and be your friend if you can remember his name, or, better yet, know the name of his son, Tom, his daughter, Sue, or when you ask sincerely about the health of his wife, Mary?

Remember His Birthday. Most firms give their employees legal holidays like Christmas, New Year's, and Thanksgiving off and pay them for it, too. Others, being more farsighted, go even further.

One of these is the Kimberly Music Industries, Inc., a Chicago corporation employing close to five hundred people. They remember an employee's birthday, send him a personal letter of congratulations signed by the president, James F. Wilkins, and give him the day off with full pay.

"Good employee relations don't cost," Mr. Wilkins says. "It

pays. Giving a man time off on his birthday and paying him for it, too, shows we pay attention to him and that we're interested in him. We consider him as being important to us as a human being and we appreciate the work he does for us. We like him as an employee and we want to keep him with us."

USE A MERIT SYSTEM FOR PROMOTION

Never Play Favorites.   Not only is it important to give credit when and where it's due, but it's also just as important not to give it when and where it's not due. Don't keep a man in your service just because he's done a favor for you and you're now obligated to him.

Office politics should play no part in the promotion of the people who work for you. A definite merit system should be used. The smartest move you'll ever make in handling your subordinates is *never accept any favors from any of them.* Don't allow yourself to be compromised. Leave that game to the politicians.

I know of no faster or surer way of destroying the morale of your people than for you to play favorites and to be partial toward a certain person or a certain group. If you favor the incompetent and inefficient, if you pass over deserving people when it comes time for promotion, you'll soon find that's all you have left on your hands to work for you: the incompetent and inefficient.

COUNSEL HIM ABOUT HIS PERSONAL PROBLEMS

This is a delicate area. You need to approach it with caution. I've asked Melvin Taylor, Industrial Relations Manager for the Kennedy Brick and Steel Company of Youngstown, Ohio, to give you some guidelines he gave me that I've found to be very helpful.

"Stick to the Personal Problems that Interfere with His Work," Mr. Taylor says. "Don't try to solve all the personal problems of the people who work for you. Just stick to helping them solve the ones that interfere with their jobs. That'll keep you quite busy enough. There are usually three ways a person can cause you a problem:

"1. He underperforms in his job, either quantity-wise or quality-wise.
"2. He interferes with the performance of others.
"3. He causes harm to his group by what he says or does.

"Unless he's causing one of these three things to happen, you can't honestly say he's a problem to you. He might have marital problems, finance problems, a hundred and one other personal problems that are bothering him, but as long as he does his job, and doesn't interfere with others, that is none of your business, *unless he asks you for help.* Then you should do your best to help him.

"You Can't Counsel Your Employee by Criticizing Him," Mr. Taylor goes on to say. "If he comes to you for advice and assistance, remember you can't help him by criticizing. He wants sympathy, understanding, and an attentive ear from you. If he has a drinking problem and comes to you for help, don't tell him he shouldn't have started drinking in the first place. That's no help at all. That's about the same as telling a person with a marital problem he shouldn't have gotten married. Makes just about as much sense.

"If You're Not the Expert, Don't Try to Be One," Mr. Taylor says in conclusion. "If you don't know the answer to his problem, then say so. Don't try to be an expert if you're not one. If a man comes to you with a drinking problem, for example, and you don't know how to help him, contact Alcoholic Anonymous. They do know how. Sometimes the best counselling you can give a person is simply to *tell him where to find the answers to solve his problems."*

GIVE HIM GOOD WORKING CONDITIONS

If you have any control over the working conditions of your people, you ought to make them as comfortable as possible. Promote good working conditions for your employees and you'll benefit in the long run by having increased efficiency.

Good lighting cuts down on eye strain; it helps get rid of safety hazards and prevents accidents. It improves the quality of workmanship and raises morale. Proper ventilation, good heating and cooling, elimination of unwanted and unnecessary noise all help improve worker efficiency by getting rid of employee fatigue.

Good housekeeping is important. No one likes to work in a filthy place. The standards of almost any organization can be judged by the cleanliness of the *employees'* washrooms.

Next time you take your car to the garage, take a look at the washroom. Not the one reserved for the customer's use. Look at the one the mechanics use. You'll be able to tell in a hurry if you want to have your car serviced there or go somewhere else.

OFFER HIM JOB SECURITY

Although this is the least important point from the employee's viewpoint, it still does mean something to him. A person is entitled to know that, as long as he does a good job, he won't be fired for some little inconsequential reason.

And you should always remember that, although this list is representative of the desires of several thousand workers, that doesn't mean that all of them put job security down in last place.

Not only that, a man's personal needs and desires can change as he grows older. When Joe Green is 23 and single, job security might be number 8 to him. When he's 48, has four children to put through college, a mortgage on his house, and a 5 year old car about to fall apart, job security can become number one to him in a hurry.

As the old man once said, "It's a lot easier to be philosophical about sex in your seventies than it is in your twenties."

Along this same line, I'd recommend you let your employees give a numerical rating to these eight basic needs and desires each year. Post these entries on a master file for each person. You can then see for yourself how his attitudes and ideas change from year to year. And you'll have an up-to-date intelligence report on every single person to help you know exactly what approach you need to use to put yourself across with him.

HOW *NOT* TO USE NEGATIVE INCENTIVES

Unfortunately, a lot of teachers, employers, managers, foremen, and supervisors seem to think that negative incentives are valuable. Negative incentives, such as punishment in the form of demotion, loss of money in penalties and fines, suspension, loss of free time, and so on, could possibly be of some value in controlling the extreme lowest level of people. Even then, I doubt it seriously.

Another thing about using negative incentives, too. You see, to threaten a person takes no effort at all on your part. It's the easy way out. But to figure out how you can motivate a person to do what you want him to do takes some brain work from you.

In the long run, though, you'll get much more out of him by using positive motivators. You simply cannot put yourself across with the people who work for you by using threats and coercion.

I, personally, have never cared for the use of negative incentives. They do not get the job done for me. Negative incentives might get the person to do the bare minimum for you because of his fear, but that's all they'll ever do. They'll never motivate him to give you his maximum performance.

And after all, that's what you really want from the people who work for you: their maximum performance. You can't get that from them by using punishment as a motivator.

12

How to Give Orders
That Always Get Results

To ACHIEVE THE BENEFITS OF ACCOMPLISHING YOUR MIS-
sion, you'll first need to give clear and concise orders. Then
you'll have to make sure your orders are understood. And you'll
need to supervise to insure that they are promptly and properly
carried out.

The wise leader makes judicious use of his subordinates to
carry out his orders effectively. If you fail to make proper use
of your people, and if you fail to use their skills and their
abilities to the utmost, you'll demonstrate a fundamental weak-
ness in your own abilities to put yourself across with others.

People respond more quickly to orders that are clear, concise,
to the point, and easy to understand. On the other hand, they
can easily become confused if you over-state your instructions
by giving them too many details. Your people will want to know
that you are available for advice and counsel if and when you
are needed. However, they'll always resent oversupervision for
they look at that as only harassment.

Individual initiative is developed within people when you
let them use their imagination in developing their own techniques to do their jobs. And that, too, is a distinct benefit for
for you. Now for the techniques.

MAKE SURE THE NEED FOR AN ORDER EXISTS

Certain administrative details in our daily lives or in our work become so routine that it's absolutely unnecessary to issue any sort of an order about them. You don't need to give your wife an order to cook supper, nor does your boss need to give you an order each morning to come to work that day.

And most of the time, the details of any business or office are handled by some sort of an established and accepted SOP (Standing Operating Procedure), whether it's a written one or not. The only time an order would be needed then would be if a change in time or procedure takes place.

For example, if you've left standing instructions with your secretary always to bring the morning mail to your desk as soon as it comes in, then you shouldn't have to tell her every single day to do that. Or if you've told the milkman to leave two quarts of milk every Monday and Thursday, that's what you'll get until you change your original order.

Every unit in the army makes up a *morning report* and sends it to its next higher headquarters. The name in itself is almost self-explanatory. It's a report that is made every morning to show the status of every officer and enlisted man in that unit. In fact, a morning report is as old as the army itself is.

Now if a newly commissioned second lieutenant were to be given command of a company, and if he were to say to his first sergeant, "Sergeant Jones, make up the daily morning report and send it to regiment," he would probably be sent to the psychiatric ward for examination. That would be the extreme example of an unnecessary order in the army.

But if the same young second lieutenant were to say to his first sergeant, "Sergeant Jones, has the morning report been sent to regiment yet?" that would not be an unnecessary order. In fact, it would not be an order at all. It would be supervision, a very important and necessary part of the lieutenant's duties and responsibilities to make sure that the job gets done.

Parents often give their children orders that are not required at all just to prove that they're the boss. I'm as guilty as everyone else, I suppose. For instance, my wife says, "Supper's ready. Please call the children." I do, and my youngest son, Larry, comes in from the game room all sweaty and dirty from playing ping-pong with his brother, Bob. He's halfway through the bathroom door to clean up when I say, "Go wash your hands." And then I wonder why he gives me such a dirty look!

So if you're wondering to yourself whether an order is necessary or not to prove you're the boss, please remember this: *If you're the boss, people already know that.* You don't have to issue an order to prove it.

But if you do need to issue an order to get the job done, do so. Don't be afraid of hurting someone's feelings by telling him what to do. If that's your job and it has to be done—then do it.

NEVER ISSUE AN ORDER YOU CAN'T ENFORCE

One of the secrets in being a successful leader and in putting yourself across with people is never to issue an order you can't enforce, make a decision you cannot support, or give a promise you cannot keep.

If people refuse to carry out your orders, if they refuse to do what you tell them to do, and if you can't back up your order and enforce it, you'll end up with a mob on your hands instead of a well-disciplined group of people.

Depending upon the person who's receiving your order, there are several different approaches you can use. One of these is to—

Ask the Person if He Can Do the Job

Harry Vaughn has one of the toughest jobs in industry. He's the last man in the management line, a production supervisor for the Gold Seal Travel Trailer Corporation in Elkhart, Indiana. He has direct charge of the employees on the assembly line. Harry calls himself a *front-line supervisor,* because he gets shot at from both sides.

"My job is the lowest position in management," Harry says. "If I were to go down just one more step, I'd be in the union.

"One of the biggest problems I had to learn how to solve when I became a production supervisor was to give orders so the men would want to obey them. In the beginning, it seemed I did everything wrong. I'd give a man a job to do that he didn't know how to do or that he couldn't possibly finish in the time I gave him to do it. As a result, things really got fouled up on my assembly line and my production fell way off.

"Then I got wise about a few things. I learned how to give an order so it would always be obeyed without question. Now I ask a man if he knows how to do a certain piece of work. If he says 'Yes,' I ask him to please go ahead and do it.

"I'll also ask him how much time he needs and when the job will be done. I accept his estimate and I hold him to it. If he misses, or if he complains about it, I remind him that *he's the one who set his own deadline.*

"If a man tells me he can't do a certain job, I ask him why not and he tells me. I then give him a certain amount of time to learn those duties. Or I ask him what he can do and when he tells me, I put him to work on that job. No matter which way a man goes, I've got him covered now. I can't lose as long as I ask him first."

Another way you can make sure your order is obeyed is to—

Show Him the Benefit He'll Gain

After World War II, thousands of ex-servicemen were interviewed by the army to find out some of the things these former GIs throught were wrong. One of the points they brought up most often was that officers should always explain *why* a particular order was being given or *why* a certain action was required if they wanted to get the best efforts out of their men.

I would carry this idea even one step further and say, "Not only should you tell a person *why* your order is being given or *why* the action is necessary, but you should also *tell him how he'll benefit* when he does as you ask him to do."

I'd also be the first to admit that this will take some real digging on your part to come up with benefits people can gain by following your order, but it can be done. What are the benefits to be gained by getting good grades in college, for instance? A better-paying job when you graduate. What are the benefits to be achieved by producing more quality work when you're on an incentive basis? More money in your pay check at the end of the week.

"Even safety programs can be revamped to stress benefits to be gained by the employees," says Mark West, Safety Director for Iowa Beef Packers, Incorporated. "We used to give a safety orientation program for our new employees called 'Plant Safety Rules and Regulations.' People just slept through the class.

"Then we rewrote the whole program, gave it a brand-new slant and took a new approach to it from the employees' viewpoint. Today, our orientation program is called 'Safety Benefits for You.' Even our old long-term employees like it so well they come back time after time to hear it again. Nobody sleeps through it any more."

Some companies also find their employees follow safety rules and regulations far better when their hourly pay is increased for each year they go without an accident. That gives a person a real incentive to obey your order when he receives a financial benefit for doing so.

USE YOUR ESTABLISHED LINE OF AUTHORITY

In the army they call it *chain of command;* in business and industry it's usually termed the *line of authority.* Some people try to soften its harsh tone by calling it the *channel of communi-*

cation. But whatever you call it, it still means the same thing. What it really boils down to is that in any outfit *each man can have but one immediate superior and that there can be only one final boss at the top of the heap.*

For our purposes here, let's call it the *line of authority;* that line through which orders and directives flow down and information and reports flow up. Now to get his orders down to the level where the actual work finally takes place, the boss may have to transmit them through a production manager to a department foreman to a shift supervisor to the production employee. The number of levels through which any order must pass will depend mainly on how complex and how wide-spread the organization is.

You should know and you should always use your established line of authority whenever you issue an order. Don't bypass your production superintendent or the production foreman and tell the shift supervisor or the production employee what to do.

And if you're not the boss, but you're one of those intermediate people I just mentioned, then you should make doubly sure that you know who your immediate superior is, who his immediate superior is, and so on right on up to the top. You must also know who your own subordinates are, for you give orders only to them, not to someone's else's subordinates. That's one of the reasons for having a definite line of authority.

Most companies and corporations have an organizational chart that clearly shows the various offices, sections, and departments, who works for whom, and exactly where and through whom the line of authority passes. Study it. Know it. You'll save yourself much trouble when you do. When you know it thoroughly, there'll be no excuse on your part for not giving your orders to the right person. Nor will there be any excuse for your taking orders from the wrong person either.

If you do bypass a level of supervision when you issue an order, you're intimating that you lack confidence in the abilities of those you've bypassed. Not only that, you may issue orders that conflict with those of that person's immediate superior. If that happens, and chances are good that it will, that person will be at a complete loss as to what to do, for no man can obey conflicting orders. It is impossible for anyone to have two bosses and satisfy either one of them.

This, then, is almost an iron-clad rule. The only exception I can think of is if there's an actual emergency such as a fire or an accident. Just make sure an actual emergency does exist before you start skipping levels of supervision and control. If you must violate this rule, then make certain that those you've bypassed are informed as soon as possible as to exactly what you've done and why.

ISSUE CLEAR, CONCISE, AND POSITIVE ORDERS

"Why don't they tell me what they want me to do? Why don't they make up their minds about what they want? Why can't someone tell me what's going on around here?"

Ever hear comments like these before from your people? Ever say the same things yourself? So have I. Many, many times.

Your ability to translate your wishes and your desires into clear, concise, and positive orders can be one of the biggest problems you have to solve. But a lot of your potential troubles will fade away and disappear if you'll just—

Use Mission-Type Orders

What is a mission-type order? Well, simply said, *a mission-type order tells a person what you want done, but it does not tell him how to do it.* The how-to is left entirely up to him.

"Using a mission-type order can bring you a multiplicity of benefits," says Jimmy Yamashiro, west coast sales manager for Oriental Imports, Incorporated, of San Francisco. "First of all, a mission-type order emphasizes results—not methods. It tells a person what you want done, but it doesn't tell him what he has to do to get those results.

"Our sales representatives can develop their own ideas when we give them quotas to meet without telling them exactly how to do it. They have to use their own imagination and ingenuity to come up with their own techniques and their own methods to increase their sales.

"I can say this. It works. Whenever you use mission-type orders, you open the door wide for your people so they can use their initiative to get the job done for you."

When You Decentralize Responsibility—You Must Also Decentralize Authority. When you use mission-type orders, you decentralize responsibility. Therefore, you must also decentralize authority so that person will be able to carry out his responsibility.

When you try to give a man responsibility without authority, you're merely passing the buck. But when you give him the authority to carry out his responsibility, then you're doing your job.

If you're his boss, you'll still retain your overall responsibility for accomplishment of the mission. You still have to supervise and see that he does his job. You can't give away your own responsibility and get by with it.

"You Can Use Mission-Type Orders to Weed Out Incompetent People," says Walter Albert, production manager for the Arizona Chemical Products Company in Phoenix. "Mission-type orders will bring out the initiative and the resourcefulness of your best people. If a person is not stimulated to do a better job for you when you use this kind of order, chances are he's not worth his pay to you at all.

"You'll find that using mission-type orders is one of the most effective ways for you to weed out the inefficient and incompetent person before he becomes a burden to you. If you do have people in your organization who can't handle this kind of an order, get rid of them. Replace them with people who can. You'll both be much better off."

DISGUISE YOUR ORDERS AS SUGGESTIONS
OR REQUESTS

If your people have any initiative whatever, you'll get far better results by using suggestions than by giving direct orders. The average person doesn't respond too well to direct commands unless he's in the army, and even then, that's no guarantee.

I have always been able to get extremely good results by asking a person to do something or by suggesting that he try it a certain way. And there's no law that says you can't use such expressions as "Why don't you try it this way? What is your idea on this? Would you be good enough to . . . I wish you would . . . do you think you can . . . when could you have it done?"

I will say that using suggestions or requests works a lot better than yelling at a person. When you yell at a man, all you're doing is inviting him to yell right back at you. That's how most arguments get started in the first place. Never raise your voice unless the person is too far away to hear what you're saying. Even then, I'd recommend you move closer before you talk with him.

"Many times the best way to get a job done that you want done is to let the other fellow think it's his own idea," says Dean Zeigler, production foreman for the Phelps Tool and Die Manufacturing Company in Omaha, Nebraska. "If you want to get something done without a lot of static and backtalk, the best thing to do is to plant the idea in someone else's head in such a way that he'll think it's his own.

"For instance, if I go out and tell one of my supervisors how we're going to revamp his whole assembly line so we can speed up production, he'll automatically be against it simply because he wasn't consulted on it or it wasn't his idea.

"To keep that from happening, I go to him first and I say, 'Joe, I was sort of wondering if we wouldn't be able to speed up production a little more if we moved the number 2 machine down to here, and if we put the cutter and trimmer over there, and . . . tell you what, Joe. How about thinking it over and give me your ideas on it in a couple of days.'

"I never say anything more about it. I don't have to. A few days later, Joe will come storming into my office and say, 'Dean, I've got the best idea in the world about how to speed up production. First we need to move the number 2 machine to here, and then . . . why don't you come on out to the assembly line, Dean, so I can show you exactly what I mean.'

"Works every time. I get what I want. Joe's happy because he's convinced himself the whole thing was his own idea. What the heck. I don't mind if he gets the credit. He does a much better job for me and the company if he does. And after all, that's what I really want from him: a better job. That's all I'm really after."

CHECK FOR UNDERSTANDING

When you issue an order, it is not only important that your order be understood, but it is also important that it be worded in such a way that it is impossible to be misunderstood.

There are three specific things you can do to find out whether your orders are being understood or not. And you should use all three of them every time you issue an order.

1. Ask them if they have any questions.
2. Ask them questions yourself.
3. Have your people repeat your oral instructions.

Ask Them if They Have any Questions.   Normally, if the average person doesn't understand exactly what you want him to do, he'll ask you questions so he can clear up any doubtful points. You can motivate him to do that simply by saying, "Are there any questions? Is there any point you don't understand?" However, if that doesn't bring a response, don't stop there. Go right on and—

Ask Them Questions Yourself.   Don't ask "Do you understand?" or "Do you have any questions?" or "Get it?" That kind of general question is a waste of time. To find out for sure if your orders are being clearly understood or not, you must ask questions like these:

> "How do you plan on doing this, Sam?"
> "How do you think you'll tackle this problem, Bill?"
> "Do you see now why this small ring goes on last?"
> "Do you understand why a constant 93 degrees is necessary?"

You must use specific questions that are direct, to the point, and relevant to the subject if you want to make sure your orders are completely understood.

Have Your People Repeat Your Oral Instructions.   I can think of no exception to this rule. So help me, the first time you break it, things'll go wrong. It never fails. If your people don't understand exactly what you want, it's absolutely impossible for you to get what you expect.

So make this a hard and fast rule. Oh, I know you may have some people who might resent this procedure. They think you think they're stupid when you ask them to repeat your orders. Just let them read Chapter 3 where we discussed that. There's also another way of getting around that problem.

You see, most of the time, even though you issue oral orders, you use notes to do so. And most of the time, your subordinates take notes. If they don't, ask them to. When you've finished, then you can say, "George, would you mind reading that back to me. I want to check *my* notes on that point."

And if he still resents it, well, he'll just have to resent it, that's all. Your job is to see that the job gets done.

CHECK FOR PROGRESS

Here is the point where so many people fail and here's why: You issue an order. Everybody understands you. You smile. You're happy. You figure you've done a good job. So you go back to your office, sit down, have a cup of coffee, and read the morning paper. All's right with the world.

Meanwhile, everything's going smoothly. Your orders are being carried out promptly and properly. You might as well go play golf this afternoon. Is all this true? No, it's not true at all. Why not? *Because an order without supervision is not an order at all.* It's only wishful thinking.

To make sure the job gets done, to make sure your order is being carried out, you must constantly check for progress by inspecting your people's work. Always remember that a person does well only that which the boss inspects. Another way of putting that is *Never Inspected—Always Neglected.*

To inspect and check a person's work without harassing him or over-supervising him is an art. It's an area in which you must go all out to put yourself across with people. To help you know how to inspect and supervise so you can really get the job done, I'd like to give you a six point checklist to use:

1. Set Aside a Specific Amount of Time Each Day for Your Inspections.   Check some phase of your operation every single working day. Never let a day go by without inspecting something. You'll soon find that Monday mornings and Friday afternoons are the let-down periods. You must bear down harder at those two times than any other to get the job done. I'm thoroughly convinced that my last two cars were built during one of those two time periods.

2. Pick Your Inspection Points Before You Inspect.   Plan your inspections ahead of time. Don't inspect in a haphazard way. Pick at least three, but no more than eight, points that you want to check in your inspection. Review these points before you inspect. Never allow yourself to get caught short. You must be the expert and the authority when you inspect someone else's work. If you can be fooled by your people and if they can bamboozle you, then you'd better stay in the office.

3. Inspect Only These Points.   Don't allow yourself to be led astray. This can become a cat-and-mouse game if you allow it to. Your people will always try to lead you away to inspect the points they've selected. Don't let yourself be led into that trap. Remember who's inspecting and who's being inspected.

Whenever a person wants to show you how good a job he's done on something, you know darned well something else hasn't been done. To inspect is to *emphasize only the points you've selected*—not the points they'd like to select for you.

4. Always Bypass Your Line of Authority.   A while ago I told you never to bypass any level of your line of authority *when you issue an order*. And that's true. But when you inspect, *you should always bypass your line of authority*. No other kind of inspection is worthwhile at all.

If you ask the foreman or the supervisor, the captain or the lieutenant how things are going, you know the answer before you ask the question. So don't ask them. Ask their subordinates. Ask the people who are actually doing the work if you want an honest and unbiased answer.

You should take the foreman or the supervisor along with you. That's a matter of courtesy. After all, you're not trying to go behind their back, play spy, and get something on them. At least you shouldn't be; you should be inspecting—not snooping.

5. When You Inspect—Don't Talk—Listen.   Remember you're inspecting to get information—not to give it out. Your purpose should be to gather data and check progress—not to tell jokes, gossip, or shoot the breeze.

You can really turn a person on with the question word of "Why?" or the uplifted eyebrow of doubt or skepticism when he tells you something. He'll go all out to make sure you do understand when you use these tactics.

6. Vary Your Supervisory Routine.   This is another trap that's all too easy to fall into. We all are creatures of habit and we like to do the same things the same way at the same day every day. Don't do it here.

Change things around constantly. Vary your time of inspection. Change your point of inspection. Scramble everything just like eggs. It helps keep your people on their toes all the time.

USE THOUGHT AND CARE IN YOUR SUPERVISION

Over-supervision will destroy the initiative of your people. They'll resent you deeply for over-supervision is an insult. You're questioning a person's abilities and intelligence if you're constantly peering over his shoulder. He'll consider it as harassment and no doubt he's right if you're always standing there.

However, under-supervision won't get the job done for you either. You can't spend all day in your cozy little office. A good way to supervise is simply to walk around a lot and look. Your presence alone can act as a powerful stimulus to do the job. *To see and be seen* is a supervisory cliché, but it's still true, and it still works, so you really ought to use it.

DO EVERYTHING YOU CAN TO HELP

This is perhaps one of the best ways to hit the happy medium in supervision. Let your people know that you're interested in helping them get the job done. That way you'll have a more logical reason for your presence.

To prove that you really mean business about helping them, don't hesitate to get your hands dirty once in a while. Get a little oil on your shirt—some grease on your nose. Your people will love you for it. It makes you a part of the team—a member of the family. I'd give you only one small word of caution here before you get completely carried away with this idea: *When the boss gets too involved in the work, he's no longer the boss.*

HAVE THE PERSON CHECK BACK WHEN THE JOB IS DONE

If the person is dependable and if you trust him implicitly, you can have him check back with you when the job is done rather than supervising him all the way through. However, even then, if the task is an extremely long or difficult one to finish, it would be best to set up intermediate check points so you can make sure the project stays on schedule.

HOLD A FORMAL CRITIQUE AND REVIEW

When a specific job is done, that is the best time to assemble everyone to congratulate them, to talk it over, to discuss the mistakes that were made, and to make plans for the next project.

A formal critique and review is a good way to get the bugs ironed out so you can get off to a fresh clean start and run a better show the next time. It's also a good way to close any project, and come to think of it—it's the best way to end this chapter, too.

13

How to Get the Best Out of People

$\mathcal{I}$N 1967, A BOOK OF MINE CALLED *How to Use the Dynamics of Motivation* * was published. It was written primarily for executives, managers, foremen, supervisors, businessmen—in fact, for anyone who has anything at all to do with supervising people. Its primary purpose was to show how to get the best out of people.

It was quite well accepted, in fact, so much, that thousands of copies have been sold, and are still selling, in the United States, and it has been reprinted in London, England, by the Heron Book Company as a *Business Leader's Handbook*.

This last chapter is sort of a thumbnail sketch of some of the high lights of that book that I knew would be useful to you in putting yourself across with people.

And whether you supervise three people or three thousand, you'll find that this chapter will help you get the best from the most valuable asset you can ever have—the individual performance of each and every one of the people who work for you. And that's a mighty big benefit.

---

* James K. Van Fleet, *How to Use the Dynamics of Motivation* (West Nyack, New York, Parker Publishing Co., 1967).

KNOW YOUR BUSINESS AND STICK TO IT

When you know your business and stick to it, you'll be able to get the best out of people. Don't try to be an expert on everything; it can't be done. Stick to your own business—not to someone else's. When you do that, you'll gain the respect, the confidence, the willing obedience, the loyal cooperation, and the full support of all the people who work for you.

And it is important that you get people to do their best for you. Anything less than that is not enough. To almost, but not quite, make the grade is merely an exercise in character building.

"The real goal of putting yourself across with your employees should be to get them to do their best for you all the time," says Jim Taylor, manager of the Dayton Rubber Company's Waynesville, North Carolina branch plant. "To achieve that goal, you must be able to reach every person in your organization in such a way that each one of them will be inspired to give his best efforts possible every minute of the working day in line with his own individual abilities. Knowing your own job, sticking to it, and then giving it everything you've got will help your employees to do that."

If you don't know your own business, your people will soon lose confidence in you. If you don't have the technical and the professional know-how it takes to do your job—if you show a lack of knowledge and skill in your work—your own employees will lose confidence in your professional abilities. When that happens, they'll lose respect for you. You'll never be able to get them to do their best for you if you're trying to bluff your way through.

So you should be well-rounded in your job, no matter how your knowledge was gathered, whether it was through education, experience, or both. And you should keep right on learning more about it every day. You'll never live long enough to know everything there is to know about your chosen profession.

This idea doesn't mean you shouldn't know and understand the jobs of the people who work for you. Not at all. That's an important part of your business to know, too. Nor does it mean you shouldn't train yourself so you'll be ready to take over your boss's job at a moment's notice. That's also another important part of your business. If you can't do that, you can bet that someone else can. If you're not ready to take advantage of that chance when it comes along, you can be sure that someone else will be.

So you see, that means if you're going to be able to supervise properly, and if you're going to be ready for promotion, you'll have to know everything there is to know about your business inside out—from the bottom to the top. There is absolutely no substitute for a knowledge such as this.

To sum up this idea of sticking to your own business, and not to someone else's, let me quote what the celebrated Roman poet, Horace, said about it a couple of thousand years ago. He said, "I attend to the business of other people, having lost my own."

And if you don't concentrate on your own affairs—if you don't stick to your own business, not someone else's—the same thing can happen to you, too.

BE HONEST WITH YOURSELF

If you're honest with yourself, you can't help but be honest with others. And honesty with other people is a must for no one likes a liar—no one likes a dishonest man.

For instance, if you're a liar, you cannot be depended on in anything you do, no matter whether it has to do with your business life or your social and personal life.

You could be a genius, yet as a person you'd be completely worthless in the eyes of other people—an abject failure. For what value is a genius who doesn't tell the truth? Unless you are honest, no one will be able to depend on you at all. You'll never be able to put yourself across with people, and it's a cinch that you'll never be able to get the best out of them if they don't trust you.

An honest man is a man of honor. He is a man of his word. He does not lie, cheat, or steal. He does not chisel. He is a man who can be trusted for he has a strong sense of personal integrity.

Personal integrity is the derivative of personal decision. It is a priceless jewel that lies within the reach of everyone who has the courage and the desire to possess it. Here are six pointers you can use to develop personal integrity and be honest with yourself so you can get the best out of people.

1. Practice Absolute Honesty and Truthfulness in All Things at All Times.   Don't allow yourself the luxury of even one tiny white lie. If you didn't have a good time at Mrs. Brown's party, you don't have to tell her that you did. Nor do you have to tell her that you didn't. A simple word of thanks to her for inviting you will be quite enough.

2. Be Accurate and Truthful in Everything You Say or Do. You must be as good as your word and your word should be your bond. When you write a personal check, your signature is a certificate that says you have enough money in your bank to cover it. Your signature on your expense account should carry the same weight. If what you're about to sign isn't the whole truth, then you simply shouldn't sign it.

3. Stand for What You Believe to Be Right.   Have the courage of your convictions, no matter what the consequences might be. Never lower your standards; never compromise your principles.

4. Accept Responsibility for Your Own Actions.   Don't try to justify your actions by comparing them with the actions of others. You end up lying to yourself when you do. If you're willing to accept the credit when you're right, you must also be ready to take the blame when you're wrong.

At Gettysburg, after Pickett's courageous charge against the center of the Union lines failed, a young Confederate officer tried to console General Lee by saying to him, "The inexcusable acts of others made failure inevitable. It is not your fault."

But General Lee refused to pass the blame on to someone else. He accepted the responsibility for the failure. "No," he replied. "That is not true; it was all my fault."

5. Duty and Honor Come First.   If you are ever tempted to compromise your principles, then place your sense of duty and personal honor above all else. If you can grasp, understand, and practice the principles of duty and honor, you cannot help but develop your own high standards of personal integrity.

6. Be True to the Man in the Glass.   There is an old poem on my desk that I read often. It has no byline and I do not know the author's name. But the last verse sums up this idea of personal integrity quite well for it says:

> You may fool the whole world down the pathway of life
> And get pats on your back as you pass,
> But your final reward will be heartaches and tears,
> If you've cheated the man in the glass.

A great many benefits will come your way when you do develop a high standard of personal integrity in your life and become completely honest with yourself. One of the main dividends that will be yours will be an improved relationship with your family, your personal friends, your business associates, and your employees. The truthful person is always respected in his home, in his community, and at his work.

If you are honest with yourself, it is impossible for you to be dishonest with others. As a far wiser man than I once said, "This above all: to thine own self be true, and it must follow, as the night the day, thou canst not then be false to any man." *

* Shakespeare.

SET THE EXAMPLE FOR THEM TO FOLLOW

To get the best out of people, you must always set the example for them to follow. There are a multitude of good character traits you ought to have to set the example for others to follow, such as dependability, enthusiasm, initiative, tact, unselfishness, and the like. However, since we're so limited by time and space, I've chosen to discuss only one, one without which it would be impossible for you to get the best out of people.

This quality is loyalty. It can do much to earn for you the confidence and the respect of your seniors, your subordinates, and your associates. Your every act should reflect loyalty to them. To develop loyalty to your people, follow these guidelines:

1. Be quick to defend your subordinates from abuse.
2. Never give the slightest hint of disagreement with orders from your superior when passing down instructions to your own subordinates.
3. Practice doing every job to the best of your abilities and wholeheartedly support your boss's decisions.
4. Never discuss the personal problems of your subordinates or your superiors with others.
5. Stand up for your people when they are unjustly accused.
6. Never criticize your superiors in the presence of your subordinates.
7. Use discretion when discussing business matters outside your organization.

FIVE PRIMARY CHARACTERISTICS
OF LEADERSHIP

You might not look at yourself as a leader, but if you're going to put yourself across with people so you can get the best out of them, you are one, whether you like it or not. There are five major characteristics which every person must possess if he is going to develop as a leader. These are the power of decision, the wisdom to plan and order, the courage to act, the ability to manage, and the ability to get things done. Let's look at each one of these now in some detail.

The Power of Decision

To get the best out of people, you must possess the power to make a sound and timely decision. You must become adept at probing a problem to find its heart.

To do this, you'll need judgment, so that after considering all the factors bearing upon the problem before you and all the ways of solving it, you will be able to come up with the best possible solution.

You should use sound logic and reasoning if you are to attain good judgment. You must use foresight so you can predict actions or reactions that will come up after your decision has been put into action.

And to attain this foresight, you should always keep this incomplete sentence in mind: "What will happen if _____?" This idea must always be uppermost in your thoughts.

The Wisdom to Plan and Order

Once your decision has been made, your next step will be to develop a detailed plan to carry it out. A usable plan must be worked out so you can get the results you want. Definite tasks must be given to specific individuals. Allocation of supplies and equipment must be made. The work of individuals and groups will need to be coordinated to insure maximum cooperation. Definite deadlines must be established for completion of intermediate steps. And your plan must always answer these questions: What is to be done? Who will do it? Where, when, and how will it be done?

Once you've fully developed your plan, you'll want to make your desires known in the form of oral or written orders. No matter how wise and complete your plan is, unless you issue your order so that it gets down to the person on the ground who is actually going to do the job, you cannot possibly expect to succeed.

The Courage to Act

Even though you have the power to make decisions and the wisdom to plan and order, you'll still never be able to achieve your goals unless you have the courage to take action when action is necessary. You must possess the courage to start, to follow up, and to see it through to the very end.

The Ability to Manage

To get the best out of people, you must develop your own capacity to manage. It is not difficult to manage when everything is going your way—when you have more than enough trained manpower, material, and money. Almost anyone can do that.

It's when things aren't perfect that your ability to manage will come through loud and clear, for the best manager is often the best improviser. It's when you don't have enough trained people, when you don't have all the equipment, money, or time that you need to do the job that your abilities to manage will really be tested. The ability to manage in times of adversity will often be one of the most distinguishing characteristics of the successful leader.

The Ability to Get Things Done

Most of the time, people are measured more by what they get done than by what they do. About the finest reputation you can build with your people (and your boss, too) is to have it said of you that *you get things done.* You'll be known as a *can-do-person,* and that's a rarity these days.

Can-do-people are always highly sought after, for they are so few in number and they're always so highly appreciated. Remember you cannot build your reputation on what you're going to do, but on what you actually get done.

The ability to get things done is not an inherent thing; it can be developed if you follow these specific guidelines:

1. Understand exactly the mission to be accomplished; the job to be done.
2. Break it down into steps or phases to identify its elements.
3. Determine the number of subordinate supervisors who are to be given authority and responsibility for each phase.
4. Determine the tools, equipment, and materials that will be needed.
5. Issue instructions to each one of your subordinate supervisors.
6. Allocate to each supervisor the manpower, materials, and equipment that he needs.
7. Arrange for coordination and cooperation between subordinate leaders.
8. Set a time to start and a time to complete your project, making sure to allow enough time *before the actual start* for your subordinate supervisors to make their own plans and issue their own instructions.
9. Let your organization go ahead with a minimum of interference from you. Use your time for supervision, coordination, and future planning.

This simple procedure will work on big projects as well as small ones. Big responsibilities can be broken down into smaller ones. Missions can be subdivided into tasks and jobs. No matter whether the job is big or small, the success in getting things done will require vision on your part to see what needs to be done; wisdom to plan and order; courage to act to gain the ends you want.

ALWAYS GIVE THE MAXIMUM YOURSELF

If you're not willing to give it everything you've got, you don't have the right to expect your people to do so. I've never known of any company or business to succeed if the boss didn't work twice as hard or long as his employees.

It's just not in the cards for you to give only the minimum and get back the maximum. Even in Reno and Las Vegas the odds are all against you on a bet like that.

Many times giving the maximum means to persevere, not to give up until the job is finally done. In fact, giving the maximum will often take a persistence that Calvin Coolidge once described in this way: "Nothing in the world can take the place of persistence. Talent will not; nothing is more common than unsuccessful men with talent. Genius will not; the world is full of educated derelicts. Persistence and determination alone are omnipotent. The slogan 'Press on!' has solved and always will solve the problems of the human race."

SPEAK EVIL OF NO ONE

I can well remember a paper weight my father used. It had three monkeys. One monkey covered his eyes, another his ears, and the last one had his hand over his mouth. The idea, of course, was to "see no evil, hear no evil, and speak no evil."

You may have seen one like this yourself. Now it may be hard for you to see no evil or to hear no evil, but at least you can practice the third idea without too much trouble—that is, to speak no evil.

For some reason, probably because we use it as a method of elevating ourselves and building up our own importance, we tend to criticize, to belittle, to defame, and to hurt other people.

To overcome this negative tendency in yourself, simply adopt a rigid policy of self-discipline: to speak evil of no one.

The best way to speak evil of no one is to have respect for the dignity of every other person. To do that, all you have to do is treat every man like a gentleman and every woman like a lady.

You may not care for a person—in fact, you might not like him much at all—but at least you should have respect for his dignity as a human being. Not only should you not contribute to idle gossip and chatter about a person, you should take immediate steps to stop it just as Earl Best, a supervisor with the Diamond Match Company, does.

"A quick way to stop people from talking behind a person's back is to call his bluff," Earl says. "For instance, when I hear people gossiping about someone, I just cut in and say, 'I don't believe what you said about George, Tom. In fact, I'm going to give you a chance to prove it, for I'm going to get George over here right now, and let you repeat your story to him!' I've never had anyone accept my offer yet, and it sure has cut down on idle gossip and rumors in the plant."

Instead of looking for the bad points in people, why not look for some good points for a change? You can always find at least one, no matter who the person is and no matter how small his good point is.

And when you do, then you can say something decent about someone. I'm sure it'll make a pleasant change in the atmosphere, even though it might come as a surprise to a lot of people.

HOW TO GET THE BEST OUT OF EVERYONE

Psychologists, psychiatrists, ministers, marriage counselors, business and management consultants, criminologists have all come to one single conclusion in this business of putting yourself across with people. The answer is that to get the best out of people, you must give your whole-hearted attention to them.

If this seems hard to believe to you, then I'd ask you only to look at some of the unhappy results that take place when a person is neglected—when no one pays any attention to him. They can range all the way from self-pity to crime.

The unwanted child, the rebellious teen-ager, the wandering wife or husband, the neurotic in the doctor's office, even the rioter in the streets or the hardened criminal in the penitentiary are all saying the same thing through their actions: *I want attention from you; pay attention to me.*

Now the average normal person you're associated with may not resort to such drastic methods, but he still wants attention, too. Here are three simple ways to give it to him so you can get him to give his best for you.

Get Your Mind off Yourself

Most of us are self-centered much of the time. Each one of us is busy trying to impress our listeners or keep ourselves in the spotlight. But if you want to make sure of paying close attention to another person, this is exactly what you must not do.

And that will take a definite effort on your part to step downstage. You'll have to forget yourself for a while and get your own hungry ego to take a back seat for a change. You have to stop trying to get attention and give it to someone else.

Don't Talk—Listen

The art of paying attention to the other person cannot possibly be practiced until you learn to zip your own lip. There's a name for the person who talks all the time—a bore. And so help me, if I had the choice of going to heaven with a bore who has his mouth open talking about himself all the time, or to the other place with some kind-hearted and interesting sinner who pays attention to me, I'd pick the kind-hearted sinner every time!

Learning to listen with everything you've got means you'll have to put aside your own selfish interests, your own pleasures, and your own preoccupations, at least, while you're listening to the other person. You must focus 100 per cent of your attention on him.

Practice Patience

Many times the best way you can practice patience is not to criticize and offer snap judgments. Often it's a matter of waiting, listening, standing by silently until the person you're paying this close but silent attention to works out the answer to his own problem.

Sure, this is tough to do sometimes, especially when it's your own children, but I know of no other way to help the person mature and grow up. This is not to say that I do not offer guidance, advice, and help when it is asked for, but in the end only one person can make the final decision, and if you're not that person, then there's really nothing more that you can do about it.

I know of no better example of patience than the parable of the Prodigal Son in which the father waited patiently for his son to attain wisdom and maturity. He did not reject his son when he returned, but, instead, welcomed him back with open arms. Would that I myself could always have that same capacity for patience and forgiveness!

THE LAST WORD

Most books on improving your relationships with people are written in a positive manner indicating what you should do rather than what you should not do. Most of mine have been written that way, too.

However, there still do seem to be times when it is easier to get a point across by saying *Don't* rather than *Do*. This is one of these rare times.

You see, you and I might not like some of the precepts laid down in the Ten Commandments nor might we appreciate being told what *not* to do.

However, at the same time I must admit that such phrases as "Thou shalt not kill; thou shall not commit adultery; thou shalt not steal; thou shalt not bear false witness . . ." seem to carry much more weight than if Moses had said, "Always preserve another man's life; be faithful to your wife or husband; always honor the rights of another man to retain his own possessions; always tell the truth. . . ."

So for a fresh, brand-new slant on how to get the best out of people, let me close this chapter and the book by giving you a list of *Fourteen Common Don'ts* you ought to keep in mind.

1. *Don't* try to set up your own standards of right and wrong.
2. *Don't* try to measure the enjoyment of others by your own.
3. *Don't* expect a uniformity of opinions in everything.
4. *Don't* fail to make allowances for inexperience.
5. *Don't* try to mold all dispositions into one like your own.
6. *Don't* fail to give ground on unimportant trifles.
7. *Don't* look for perfection in your own actions.
8. *Don't* worry yourself and others about what cannot be changed.
9. *Don't* fail to help everybody wherever, whenever, and however you can.
10. *Don't* think something is impossible to do just because you can't do it.
11. *Don't* believe that all the truth is only that which your finite mind can grasp and understand.
12. *Don't* fail to forgive the weaknesses of others.
13. *Don't* judge by some outside quality when it is really that within that makes the man.
14. *Don't* take yourself too seriously.